Foreword By Pat

Every Day
is
Game Day!

"Stop Practicing at Life… The Clock is Already Running"

Tim Enochs
Master Coach – Building Champions, Inc.

Erik,

Live like a Champion

because

Every Day is Game Day

Jim
5-16-08

Table of Contents

——∞∞∞——

Endorsements

―⚬⚬⚬―

" An Olympic medalist doesn't become a champion in a day. It's the result of living everyday like a champion. The stories within the pages of this book will inspire and equip you to live like a champion! Buy this book, read it, apply it, and begin a lifetime of living like a champion."
- John Maxwell – Author of The 21
Irrefutable Laws of Leadership

"Tim has written a wake-up call for people who are waiting for life to happen. Anyone who strives to be the person God intended them to be will find inspiration and practical advice in this book."
Patrick Lencioni, Author of The Five
Dysfunctions of a Team

"Our decisions determine the outcomes of our lives. Each second by second decision has the ability to impact our lives either positively or negatively for unknown durations. The issue is that most of us do not truly understand the brevity of our days and as a result, live out our days making decisions based upon the false assumption that there will always be tomorrow. But will there? Coach Tim Enochs does an excellent job helping readers to better understand that there is no second chance at today. We get no do-over's. Today is Game Day and how we live it will determine what kind of legacy we leave."

- Daniel Harkavy
CEO of Building Champions, Inc.
Author of *Becoming a Coaching Leader*

"Tim offers good practical insight into developing a winning plan so that you can live every day like a champion. Champions prepare to win; it's the Law of the Dress Rehearsal. If you want to become a champion then this book is a must read."

- Todd Duncan – Author of *High Trust Selling* and *Time Traps*

"The title says it all: *Every Day is Game Day*. Ever the consummate life coach, Tim captures the essence of what present actions, if practiced, will forever change your future. Read this book because everyday is "Game Day." You can be a winner, a champion."

- Dennis Worden – Crown Financial

"Every Day is Game Day has inspired and motivated me to reach my potential as a champion and take this "game" called life to the next level."

- Lisa Moody – Project Coordinator
– Coordinated School Health

"Tim takes proven fundamentals that are spiced with new and inspired ideas, writing them in a language we can all understand. Tina, my wife, couldn't put it down. She said, "I CAN do this!" We can't make time so we must be confident in our choices and priorities while being able to evaluate a

day at a time. Can't change and shouldn't complain about yesterday... just play our "A" game today."
- Gary Madden – President JMS Metal Services, Inc.

"In Tim's book, *Every Day is Game Day*, he challenges the reader to make every moment count by living it out as a champion. This is a "must read" for anyone who cringes at the word "mediocrity". Within these pages are some very practical tools to help champions finish strong when it counts the most—Every Day!"
- David Hughes – Sr. Pastor, Gregory's Chapel

What People Are Saying about Game Day Centered Presentations

———⚬⚬⚬———

"Tim absolutely knocked it out of the park. This is a great way to introduce coaching and life on purpose. Thanks Tim. Can't wait to have you back again."

-Brian – Sandusky, OH

"The session you conducted with my group, I am not exaggerating, was fantastic. I must share with you that I was initially somewhat apprehensive about having my sales team in an all day meeting as you know how hard it is to keep 100% highly commissioned sales people focused. The training session was well organized and targeted exactly what we had discussed I wanted the group to walk away with. The feedback from the group after the meeting was ALL POSITIVE, which is amazing. They are using the tools, and I am currently working with the group on fine-tuning their projects and disciplines. Word has spread about the success of our meeting as I have gotten emails from other managers wanting information about the session. Thanks again for a productive and worthwhile day."

Jan -Los Angeles

"Thank you so much for your "Game Day" presentation at my On-Site. I have received nothing but rave reviews from every person in attendance. You created a fun environment for each participant, drawing them into a dialogue while inspiring them (and me) to reach for new heights. Besides the presentation being inspiring, it was also presented at a pace that made time fly while achieving maximum impact. When I look back over the last 3 years of working to build deep and meaningful referral partnerships, this one event stands out and the best decision I ever made. Thank you so much for your time and willingness to come all this way. You made a huge difference!"

Candi - Tacoma, WA

"I just wanted to say "Thank you" again for inviting me to the class last Friday. I was so glad I was able to bring my assistant Brandi as well. She hears me talk about visions, goals, business plans etc. and it was nice for her to hear it in a fabulous presentation. It has motivated both of us to freshen up our goals and work on a new business plan.
The class came at a great time - it was something I needed to be reminded of again. If Tim ever comes back again, I would love to attend and bring some of my agents too. I have to say, that this class was the most helpful thing a lender has ever done for me. Thank you for including me on this presentation!"

Julie – Boise, ID

Introduction

⊶⊶⊶

The original idea for this book was birthed from the aftermath of 9/11/01. On that fateful morning, although many lost their lives, many were saved because of the valiant efforts of heroes who woke up that morning with no idea that they would do anything heroic that day. However, in the weeks, months and years leading up to this day, these brave men and women, who were first responders in New York City and Washington D.C., had been preparing and training themselves to be ready to save others... they had been living and preparing like champions. They were On Call for "Game Day"... and 9/11/01 was certainly "Game Day" for the United States of America.

As I developed the thesis for this book, I realized that we should all be preparing for something... that something is to live like a champion every day... to live like Every Day is Game Day. Every day is special. Every Day is Game Day! Game Day is that day in which all of the past culminates with present actions to forever change the future. Today is Game Day!

Within the pages of this book, you will find stories of famous and not so famous people living on purpose every day. Although there is no secret pill or silver bullet, I firmly believe that if you read this book and complete the Power Plays at the end of Chapters 1-11, you will be surprised by the positive changes in your life. This book is written for you, but I have even been challenged by my own words throughout the following pages. The simple truths you are about to read can help you transform your life into that of a consistent and true champion.

I could have never written this book alone... it was accomplished only with the support and encouragement of many. I thank God for inspiring me and giving me the words to write and favor with so many people during the process. I would specifically like to thank my awesome wife and the best two kids in the world for their patience and support throughout the process... my wonderful mom and dad (I can't say enough about the hours mom invested in helping me with this book), Daniel Harkavy (it would take another book full to thank you bro), Barry Engelman (a true "grafted in" Southern Gentleman and Mr. Mount Everest) , Jack Countryman (The Messenger), Chyna Ward (the jewel in the crown of Ole Miss football), Coach David and Karen Cutcliffe, Patrick Lencioni (thanks for the awesome sub-title), Amy Hiett (your support was incredible), Pat Williams (what an inspiration), Dennis Worden (your heart is incredible), Maury Davis (Mr. Purpose), Randy Carter, Linda Eggers, Gary and Tina (is this a sports book?) Madden, Lisa Moody, Laura DeVries (my incredible assistant coach), Dominique Defrancisci (incredible author support at Xulon Press), David Hughes (who encouraged me to "Dig Deep"), Katie Hoffman, Meghan Fitzgerald, Todd Duncan (for The Power To Be Your Best and for introducing me to Daniel Harkavy), and John Bowers, who along with my Uncle Jerald Hamm, taught me so much about people. Thank you!

I dedicate this book to the five most important people in my life, my totally awesome wife Laura, my two wonderful children, Adam and Bethany, and my incredible mom and dad, Joan and JB. Thank you for who you are and for everything you mean to me! I am so blessed!

- Coach Tim Enochs

-Foreword by Pat Williams

This is a book about consistently living like a champion in the game of life! *Every Day is Game Day* is about achieving and living the life you want… every day. As the Senior Executive Vice President for the Orlando Magic, I can tell you that championships are won and lost one game at a time. Living your life as a champion works the same way… you do it one day at a time. Each year, in the NBA, we are given a schedule that tells us who and where we will be playing throughout the regular season. We call the specific dates on the schedule *Game Day*. The rest are called "off" days or "travel days". Each annual schedule represents a season. The games won and lost do not carry over from one season to the next.

Life, on the other hand, offers a similar schedule; we call it the calendar. Unlike our basketball schedule, there are no off or travel days in life; every day is Game Day! There is no day in life that doesn't count in the won and loss column and, although there are seasons in life, wins and losses do carry over throughout the seasons of life. That's why it is so important to live like a champion every day.

In "Every Day is Game Day", my friend Tim, a life and business coach with Building Champions, has defined Game

Day as being that day in which all of the past culminates with present actions to forever change the future. When you think about it, there's just no better way to define it. Tim clearly states that everything we did or didn't do yesterday affects today, and everything we do or don't do today affects tomorrow. That's why we are compelled to live like a champion every day... because "Every Day is Game Day"!

Throughout the pages of this book you will find insight and application for becoming and living like a champion every day. You will learn a unique and enlightening definition for what procrastination really is; you will learn how to use it to your advantage rather than allowing it to negatively impact your life. You will read stories of famous and not so famous people overcoming obstacles and becoming champions. Although everyone is different, there are strategic and specific natural laws that if understood and followed will allow you to be a champion in life as well as your vocation.

In this book, Tim dispels the myth of time management. You will read that time management is not only an oxymoron but also a myth. You can't manage time any more efficiently or effectively than you can manage the traffic, or weather for that matter. Tim will show you that you can, however, manage yourself around priorities. When it comes to investing your time, it all comes down to priority management.

As you read the ensuing pages you will learn how to take what you already know and begin the process of living like a champion every day. You will be introduced to the 4-Dimensional Vision Process for making your vision become reality. Obviously there are gaps between where we all are today and where we want to be tomorrow, or some other day in the future. This book details a process to close those gaps. When the gaps are closed, you have achieved your goal.

You are about to discover a process that will give you a very winnable game plan for your life and vocation. Champions understand that life is a journey, and that successful completion of that journey involves more than just winning a victory here and there. It is about setting yourself up to win every day because every day truly is Game Day! Today is Game Day and you are holding in your hands a remarkable tool to help you put together championship seasons in your life.

The lights are on, the camera is rolling, the scoreboard is set, and expectations are high because it's Game Day! The difference between mediocrity and championship living is entirely up to you!

How to use end of chapter Power Plays

⸺❀⸺

At the end of each chapter are Power Plays developed to help you walk through the process of living like a champion. Always read the chapter prior to starting work on the Power Plays. The chapters break the ground and the Power Plays are the seeds that are planted.

Many of the Power Plays conclude with suggested books to read. These books can be read in conjunction with following the Power Plays at the end of each chapter. However, the suggested books to be read are only an enhancement to the specific activities for each set of Power Plays and can be read later. Reading does not have to occur in big chunks. A person reading only 10 pages per day would read 3,650 pages in one year. You can do the math; that could equate to a little over a book each month. How many books did you read last year? The articles, and recordings to listen to, are very important to the process at the end of each chapter and should not be delayed.

The Power Plays will help put you in the position to live a healthier, stronger, and more productive life. However, there is only one guarantee: the only Power Plays guaranteed not to help, are the ones not completed. The Power Plays are not difficult in nature; yet they can be very powerful in producing positive results in your life and business - the return on investment could blow you away!

CHAPTER 1

Champions Live Every Day Like A Champion
(...because they know Every Day is Game Day in the game of life!)

———⧟———

S top practicing at life... the clock is already running! Today is Game Day! It's time to get in the game and live like a champion right now. There are no excuses. There is no valid reason for you not to live like a champion every day.

Consider Patrick Willis... by the time he was six years old, his mom had taken his two youngest siblings Ernicka and Detris and left Patrick and his younger brother Orey behind with their dad. His dad, Ernest, was a loving father at times while exhibiting negligent and sometimes abusive behavior at other times. The negligent and abusive behaviors were brought on because of addiction to alcohol and drugs. By age 10, Patrick was working part-time jobs to help support the family. At times his dad would ask him for money to pay the utility bill only to use it to support his habits.

Patrick could have been another statistic left behind in the dust of severed relationships and addictive behavior from a father who struggled with his own challenges... but there was something different inside this young man. Patrick Willis is a champion! He pressed on in spite of his circumstances and opportunities to hide behind excuses. He found an escape through playing sports. Although he has natural talent and is such a gifted athlete, he persevered in sports as he did in life. Many times he played injured, but when he was on the field he gave it everything he possibly could.

He found success in several sports, but settled on football where he earned a scholarship to play in one of the most powerful conferences in the nation. He became an All-American and won several other awards. In spite of the success he found in sports, there were still challenges. During his junior year in college, he played hurt most of the year. He played with pain during a season in which he suffered with a partial AC joint shoulder separation, a broken middle finger, as well as a broken foot. In an interview with Chrissy Mauck for the San Francisco 49'ers, he said: "The foot hurt so bad, it was just crazy pain.... I just pushed through it." In that season he was selected as an All-American.

During the interview, Chrissy learned that it was ultimately the foot injury that prevented Patrick Willis from leaving college his junior year to pursue a career in the NFL. Still, more adversity was to come for this young man. During the summer prior to his senior year in college, Patrick's younger brother Detris, a budding athlete in his own right, tragically died in an accidental drowning while swimming with friends.

Patrick told Chrissy that there were many times that he could have said: "...this is no fun. I don't have my mama. My daddy does drugs and drinks. I lost my brother. I'm through. I want to quit." However, he concluded by saying: "But that's not who I am. I'm someone who is going to fight through it, no matter what." He did... on Saturday, April 28, 2007, Patrick's cell phone rang with a call from the San

Francisco 49'ers, notifying him that they were drafting him as the 11th pick of the 2007 NFL Draft! So what's holding you back from living like a champion every day?

(Patrick's full story can be found in a link at www.gamedaychampions.com)

Too many people go through life waiting for just the right time, or feeling, or whatever, to start (or stop) doing what they need to start (or stop) doing. Your life is what it is today, good or bad, because of past decisions, decisions to take certain actions and not take others. If you don't like the way things are, the good news is that you can start doing something about it right now! You can have the life you want. The first step starts with the decision to change... the decision to stop practicing and live like today is the most important day of your life. Are you ready?

Think about it like this... If your life were an open book for everyone to see, would it be a study in futility or a play-book for champions? The truth is that your life, as well as mine, is an open book that is read everyday by a countless number of people. It has been said that we are surrounded by a great cloud of witnesses. These people can include people who will learn from our example... good or bad. Of course, there are areas that we can hide from other people. However, in the end, the reality is that our actions or lack of action bears fruit... and we are known by our fruit. Our fruit hangs there out on the limbs of our life in clear view... we are all standing pretty much naked for the entire world to see. Do you want your life to be the playbook for champions, or the study in futility? It's your choice.

Even more important is the fact that we know the truth about ourselves. Knowing that truth either inspires us to be all that we are created to be, or drives us to pose. Posing is simply defined as pretending to others, and even to ourselves at times, that we are something that we are not.

Are there any areas in your life where you are posing? Posers constantly live with the fear of being "found out" or discovered. This is the beginning of a nasty cycle that promotes even more posing. Some people are really good posers; they are comfortable with it because they have been practicing at it for so long. It's like getting comfortable paying the minimum balance on a credit card. Little by little the balance grows until the minimum balance is more than the person can pay. The same is true with posing; the end result is that it drains you until there is nothing left to give. That cycle can be broken; and I will show you how.

If you don't like the current "truth" about your life, or if you feel some areas just need to be tweaked, there is good news! Things can change. You can bring about that change. You can become a new you... the you that you want to be... the you that you were created to be! Yesterday is gone and tomorrow can be better... today is your Game Day. Today is your day to stop playing around, only practicing at life, and start living like a champion... today is Game Day!

All American Quarterback / All American Boy

As daylight began to cut through the darkness hovering over the Atlantic Coast, the Sunshine State of Florida was poised for the beginning of a new day, a day in which the people of Florida, along with the rest of the nation, would witness lightning strike in the same place for the second time. It was a perfect day to enjoy any outside activity. The temperature was 72°F, there was a gentle breeze blowing and the sky was as blue as the ocean. The date was October 4, 2003, and it was **Game Day!**

You don't have to be a sports fan, or even like sports at all, to know that there are some places and some days that are just special... this place and this day was special.

The atmosphere in "The Swamp", home of the University of Florida Gators football team was filled with electricity... the stage was set for the lighting that was about to strike. Gator football is rich in tradition; the Florida Gators had finished inside the Top 25 in final national rankings for 13 consecutive years, which was the third longest active streak in the country for any college football team. The Gators were about to play an unranked opponent on a field where, since losing to Ole Miss in 1989, they had won 58 straight games against unranked teams. That loss in 1989 was the first lighting strike.

This game was another sellout; 90,101 raving fans made their way into the stadium; some had the "Fighting Gator" mascot painted on their faces, orange and blue Florida banners decked the stadium walls, and all around the stadium you could see the outstretched arms of thousands doing the infamous *Gator Chomp* using their arms to mimic the massive opening and closing of a gator's jaws. The *Gator Chomp* is intended by Florida Gator fans to intimidate the opponent and their fans. The currently unranked Ole Miss Rebels, with Eli Manning as quarterback, weren't intimidated. They were poised to step on the field and play like champions with no inhibitions because they had been preparing for this day like every practice day was Game Day!

Lightning was about to strike *The Swamp* in a way that no one wearing orange and blue expected... It had been 14 years and history was about to repeat itself.

Months before the season started, Ole Miss Quarterback Eli Manning had elected to remain in school and play his senior year of college football, just as his brother Peyton did at Tennessee. Passing up the prospect of a sizable NFL contract and signing bonus for another year to play at the college level with no pay is a decision that is made in the heart, not the wallet. Eli Manning made that heart-decision and came back to school with the intention of leading his team to a championship during his senior year... that meant winning tough road games in the power packed Southeastern Conference... including doing the unthinkable in "The Swamp".

That's exactly what this Ole Miss Rebel team did! With 76 seconds remaining in a tightly contested game, and Florida holding on to a razor thin 17-13 lead, quarterback and team captain Eli Manning had led his team on a 50 yard 8 play drive climaxed by a Vashon Pearson one-yard plunge into the end zone for the go ahead score... it was now Ole Miss 20 – Florida 17. The victory was sealed with 29 seconds to go in the game when junior safety Eric Oliver intercepted a pass by Florida quarterback Chris Leak at the Ole Miss 27 yard line. Lighting had struck in the same place, *The Swamp*, twice in the span of 14 years. Florida had been defeated at home by an un-ranked team...the same team that had defeated them 14 years ago.

Winning that game was the spark that ignited an explosive Cinderella season that saw Ole Miss move on to be SEC West Co-Champions with eventual National Champion LSU, and win the Cotton Bowl against a tough Oklahoma State Cowboy team in Dallas, Texas on January 1, 2004. The season ended with Ole Miss ranked 13th in the nation posting their best record and highest ranking in decades.

In March 2004, Eli Manning was chosen as the number one draft pick in the 2004 NFL Draft. He had led his team to a championship, and was presented with a multi-year, $54 million, contract with the New York Giants. However, although this Cinderella story has a great ending, there were certainly bumps along the road to greatness.

Live, Play, and Win Like a Champion Every Day

It all started to take shape when Eli, as an all-American senior quarterback in high school, made the decision to sign a letter of intent, attend Ole Miss, and play for the Rebels. He had multiple offers to play for other major college football programs … he had the pedigree and natural talent to be a champion… expectations were high. Eli Manning could have played anywhere in the country but he went with his heart.

Growing up, he had always been an Ole Miss fan. His dad, Archie, who played for Ole Miss in the late 1960's and early 70's, was the favored son of Ole Miss football… the speed limit on campus is 18 (Archie's former jersey number), and the trophy room in the school's athletic department is even named in his honor. Not only was his dad a "big man on campus", Eli's mother, Olivia, had been homecoming queen at Ole Miss during her years as a student on campus. The stage was set for Archie's son to make a name for himself on campus.

Ole Miss had a new coach by the name of David Cutcliffe, a man the family knew well and deeply respected. The choice was clear; Ole Miss was the place for Eli Manning.

Leading his beloved team to a championship, and then being selected as the number one draft pick in the NFL draft was indeed a story book ending; but, as story book endings go, there is more to this story than arriving on campus with high expectations and living happily ever after.

With all of his pedigree and natural talent, the truth is that when Eli Manning arrived on campus for the first time as a college student, not only was he a highly-recruited all-American high school quarterback, he was an All-American boy. If you've ever stepped onto a major college campus, you know that every All-American boy (or girl) has the potential to easily get distracted during that overwhelming freshman year in college. Eli got distracted.

This distraction could have been the beginning of the end for a quarterback who had the potential to be the best in the country; but it wasn't. It was the beginning of something very special. It was an opportunity to learn that in the game of life, "Every Day is Game Day"! Eli had his mom, his dad, and two brothers who loved him deeply; he also had a head coach that cared more about him as a person than as a player. He had a coach who cared more about who he was becoming than what he could do on the field; someone who wanted to help him first live like a champion so he could then play and lead his team to a championship.

Ole Miss Head coach, David Cutcliffe, who had been offensive coordinator and quarterbacks coach at the University of Tennessee, had been instrumental in coaching Eli's older brother Peyton to greatness. He knew Eli could be just as good. There seemed to be one missing link: the focus needed to live every day as Game Day.

Learning to Focus Like A Champion

Eli, like any potential champion, had to be focused in order to realize his full potential. One day "Coach Cut", as he is known among the Ole Miss faithful, called Eli into his office for one of those intense coach / player "get with the program" conversations. In his wisdom, Coach Cut asked Eli one question that would forever change, not only his life, but the direction of a major college football program nestled in the rolling hills of Oxford, Mississippi.

Coach Cut said: "Eli, you have a choice. You can stay here and play out your time having fun in college and be pretty good; or you can be a big time college football quarterback and lead this team somewhere special in the years ahead." He continued, "The decision is yours, but I don't want to know your answer today… I want you to really think about it and come back in two days to let me know your decision." Eli did just that.

In two days he reported back to Coach Cut and told him that he wanted to be a big time college football quarterback and lead his team somewhere special. At that point Coach Cut said: "Alright, starting today I am going to coach you like a big time college football quarterback and I am going to expect you to act like one."

That was the turning point. From that day forward there was no quarterback in college football more focused or prepared for games than Eli Manning. No longer was he just living for a Saturday afternoon college football game on the schedule; with a champion's heart, he was living every day as if it were Game Day... because for him every day was Game Day! Although the potential to get distracted was still present, he was a changed young man. He was focused and prepared. He grew as a leader. He became a big time college quarterback, and as you know, he led his team somewhere special in the years after that conversation with Coach Cut. Although Coach Cut and Eli Manning have both moved on, they left a legacy for the entire campus and fan base that was impacted by one student athlete who realized that every day was Game Day, and a wise coach who led him in that direction.

Life is the Season – Every Day is Game Day

Eli understood that champions live *Every Day Like It Is Game Day* – every practice counts... every play counts; there are no goof-off days for champions! Every day counts! He understood that life is the season and every day we have on this earth is Game Day... **Today is Game Day!**

It's Not About Sports

That phrase **Today Is Game Day** can be heard on crisp autumn Saturday afternoons on college campuses from coast to coast, from Michigan to Mississippi. Fans stream on to college campuses around the nation hours before their favorite teams take the field for competition. Just as in "The Swamp" in Gainesville, Florida, and across the country, even the toss of a coin can be exciting when thousands of people crowd into a stadium to watch 22 guys move an inflated pigskin up and down a 100-yard field!

"**Today is game day!**" can be heard in basketball arenas, baseball stadiums and on soccer fields around the world. In fact, it could be said that the phrase *Game Day* takes on a life of its own. My guess is that when you read those two words, at least if you are a sports fan, memories come to your mind of *Game Days* gone by… thoughts may rush through your head of *Game Days* to come. I even catch myself drifting off into thoughts of recent wins by my favorite teams and the anticipation of additional wins on the horizon. I have to force myself to pull my mind back to the present task at hand… writing this book. I could dream about *Game Day* all day every day… but if I ever want to win in this game called life… I have to wake up!

It's not about sports… it's about my life and what I want to accomplish. It's about everyone around me. It's about everything I think, say or do. Never again do I want to miss an opportunity because I wasn't living like a champion every day!

Yesterday is History – Tomorrow is Still to Come

It is easy to focus on the past, or to look to the future just thinking about the way things were, the way they might have been, or the way things may become. It takes focus to realize that yesterday is history and tomorrow is still to come. **Today is Game Day!**

"The way things might have been if I had only…" is a statement that I want to avoid saying tomorrow about today. I have to realize that yesterday is gone, and the only value in thinking about yesterday is what I learned that will help me live, or play, better today. The only good I can gain by thinking about tomorrow is in the development of a great game plan. *Game Day* is all about taking intentional action today. Learning from yesterday and planning for tomorrow should be my only concern about days gone by or days to come. Today is the only day I hold in my hand... it's the only day upon which I can exercise my will. I can take action today to have a positive impact on tomorrow!

One Day on the Calendar

Game Day **is not a game on the schedule... it is a day on the calendar... it's TODAY!** Think about it like this: *Game Day* **is that day in which all of the past culminates with present actions to forever change the future. Everything I did or did not do yesterday affects today and everything I do or do not do today affects tomorrow. Therefore, I learn from yesterday, plan for tomorrow and live like a champion today!**

Every day is *Game Day*! That mindset should affect everything I do today. There is no "off day"! Today is the day I have anticipated. Today is that day I referred to yesterday when I said I would start (or stop) doing certain things *tomorrow*. Today is yesterday's tomorrow. Today is the day I will remember tomorrow when I say "If I had only... (done)... yesterday." Today is tomorrow's yesterday. **Today is** *Game Day*!

As I said at the beginning of this chapter, you don't have to be an athlete or even like sports to gain an understanding and learn a fresh approach to winning the most important game you will ever play: **the game of life!**

This book will inspire you to squeeze everything vital out of today. It will become evident to you that **Today is Game Day in the game of life...** and how you live today will affect how you live the rest of your life! Your future, to a great extent, is the sum of your choices... winning in the season of life is all about making wise choices and taking appropriate action; it's about gaining every victory I can today.

On the following pages we will explore potential and procrastination, vision and victory, pretenders, players and champions. We will take an insider's look at some well-known stories of victory. You will also be introduced to stories of lesser-known triumphs that have the potential to inspire and prompt you to take appropriate action that will prepare you to **live every day like a champion!**

As you read you will learn, not only the concepts, but how to apply championship-living principles in your life. You will be given *Power Plays* at the end of each chapter (also found at www.gamedaychampions.com) that you can apply in your life that have the potential to lift you higher than you have ever been before, levels you may have previously considered to be unattainable.

<u>Smooth Jazz</u>

When I was nine-years-old, I started taking piano lessons; mostly because it seemed like a fun-idea to play the piano. That was a *head-decision*, not a *heart-decision*. I practiced because I had to, not because I really wanted to become an accomplished pianist; so, I never got past *book three*. That's after five years of lessons! The problem was that it was five years of lessons one year at a time. I would quit and start again in *book one*. By the way, I eventually became a master of *book one*.

When I was in the sixth grade, I decided that I wanted to be in the band and I wanted to play drums. It would be cool to play drums... drummers are just cool people. One problem with this idea was that almost every other boy my age thought that it would be cool to be a drummer, too. Since there were a limited number of drum openings (which were already spoken for), I chose trumpet because I thought playing trumpet would be a *blast.*

Trumpeting was just another head-decision, not a heart-decision. You can imagine what happened. My parents rented a trumpet for me and I showed up for band. That was the problem — I only showed up for band. I didn't practice. I faked my way through band until the director asked each trumpet player to play his part by himself! Oops! I was caught! I had been a *trumpet-pretender.* It was one of the most embarrassing days of my life! I felt like a sixth grade failure! The failure, however, was not because I couldn't play the trumpet. I failed because I made a head-decision instead of a heart-decision. I never really knew whether I could play trumpet or not. In fact, I never really discovered whether I could play piano or trumpet because I had failed to make a heart-felt commitment. It just wasn't in my heart.

It wasn't until my freshman year in high school that I decided to try the band thing again. Many of my friends were in band and I wanted to "belong", and be part of something bigger than myself. At that point I was faced with a familiar dilemma. What will I play? Then it hit me like a crescendo! Saxophone! The desire was there and I made the *heart*-felt *decision* to play saxophone. That was one decision that I would never regret. Even today, as I am sitting and writing at a table in the back corner of "The Daily Grind" (a very cool place to write), the music playing in the background is the smooth groove of saxophonic splendor, and I am still jazzed by that sweet sound. It has become part of the very fabric of my life. That's the difference in a head decision and a heart-felt commitment.

My first step was to convince my parents that I was serious this time. That was easy. I am blessed with parents who have always believed in me and supported me in areas that interested me. The next step was to talk to the band director. Thankfully it wasn't the same band director from the sixth grade. Jim Godsey was the band director and Mike Winslow led the beginning band; they were both supportive and I was ready to scale new heights.

I had found my heart in music! My attitude had been reborn! This time I practiced, and practiced, and practiced because I wanted to. My saxophone and I were ready to treat every day as if it were Game Day!

I soon graduated from beginning band into "the real band". I had arrived! Our band was divided into sections for each instrument. For the saxes it was first and second section. The best player was first chair in the first section, with the second best being in first chair in the second section. The third best player was seated in the second chair of the first section and so on down to the chair where I sat (last chair in the second section). That's right, I had arrived, but as it related to band, I was in last place... but I wasn't quite finished. I wanted more! Practice became more intense and my purpose became clear. I wanted to be first chair in the first section by my senior year, and that's exactly what I did. In three short years I was seated in the number one spot for saxophones in our band! I wasn't given that chair; I earned it! Playing the saxophone was a heart-felt commitment.

I was offered scholarships to play saxophone in the bands of at least seven universities. I had made the big time (at least in the realm of high school saxophonists). The difference had more to do with heart-felt desire and commitment than it did with natural talent. We will discuss more about that in the Chapter 3 "From Life Sentence to a Life On *Purpose*".

Today, twenty-seven years later, I still play sax for the worship team at our church, as well as for weddings and funerals. I've even played at a couple of Christmas parties. Although weddings and Christmas parties are more fun than funerals, I am honored that people respect my playing ability as final respects are paid to their loved ones. Friends have asked me to promise them that I would play at their funerals.

Why? Not because I was a *born-musician*, but because I discovered my purpose in music (to play the saxophone) and applied myself to excellence in that area. You can too! You can discover your purpose in key areas of life and apply certain principles of excellence to the extent that you are living every day like a champion. In time you will find yourself in the first chair of your chosen field!

I am not a natural born champion; neither are any of the champions I know. We have all had past successes and failures. Don't let any past failures hold you back! Believe me, if past failures could hold a person back, I would be so far back I couldn't even see the end of the line. Let all of that go. Get past it and start fresh today.

Throughout this book I will coach you though the process that has worked for me, and thousands of others we have coached at Building Champions. I will be giving specific action plans (Power Plays) that will help you, not only to apply the principles, but also thrive in the process. You will feel good about yourself even before others notice the difference in you. Change is, at first, an *inside-job*. Then, whatever is on the inside, will manifest itself outwardly. I call that fruit. Your fruit can be good.

This is not another *feel-good* or positive thinking book. It's a book about the application of principles; principles that will help you win those games in *The Swamp* against rivals and obstacles that presently seem unconquerable. Get ready to take first-chair in everything you do!

Champions don't sit on the bench or settle for second place. Champions get in the game and live every day like it's *Game Day*! Champions stop practicing at life… they realize that today is the day to play like a champion because the clock is already running.

Do you want to be a champion in your own game of life, and take your team, friends, family and yourself somewhere special in the years ahead? If you do… Read On!

If not, I wish you well as you ride out your time sitting on the bench of mediocrity...

Power Plays – Chapter 1

- Think back to the stories about Patrick Willis and "The Swamp"… Write a paragraph describing a major victory in your life (or the life of someone you know). Describe, in detail, the challenge and how it was overcome.

- Write another paragraph describing a current challenge or battle you are facing that you really want and need to win. What will need to happen for you to win?

- Now, write a paragraph or two describing how you are overcoming this challenge and how winning the battle will positively impact your life and the lives of those around you.

CHAPTER 2

In the Beginning, There Was Desire and Potential

---∞∞∞---

D esire and potential are precursors to the discovery and pursuit of purpose. No one has ever discovered his / her purpose or truly attempted to live according to that purpose without first having desire co-mingled with potential. In the following pages you will begin the process of discovering your purpose by understanding the power of the desire and potential that you already possess. The one common denominator, regardless of age, race, gender, IQ or nationality, is that people are born with desire and potential.

When a baby is born, both desire and potential are present, although neither is fully understood. However, I do believe that both are innate. If you are a parent, or have ever seen proud parents of a newborn, you know that the preeminent thought on the minds of each parent has to do with the desire and potential of that newborn baby. Many hopeful parents have the thought, at least in passing, that this baby could be a future national leader. This baby could find the cure to cancer... or the common cold. They desire to give their child every opportunity to fulfill that potential. There is so much promise in that new life, and so much desire on the part of the parents to help fulfill that promise, that it makes you wonder why every baby doesn't grow up to be a successful adult. Sadly, somewhere along the way "assumed reality" sets in and everyone seems to "come back down to earth"; desire succumbs to resignation or suspended animation and potential is never fully understood or acted upon in such a way that it could be fully realized. However, it doesn't have to be that way. Desire and potential are two of the best friends that one can have.

Let's look at desire first. Have you ever been on a long flight with a crying baby seated within 20 rows of you? If you have, you probably have had the following thought: "Why don't they do something to make that baby stop crying?" On one particular flight, I don't know what I would have done without my *BOSE* noise-canceling headset! I considered that headset to be one of my best investments ever. Something caused a baby to exercise her lung potential, and that something can be defined as an *unfulfilled desire*. The baby's only response to the unfulfilled desire was to wail her discomfort. She couldn't articulate clearly what the desire was, or how her parent might help address her need, and there was no possible way for that baby to practice self-help to fulfill that desire, so she cried, and cried while everyone else cringed at being locked in a chamber of screams at 30 thousand feet... I sat back and listened to some smooth jazz.

The first thought was that an unfulfilled appetite drove the unfulfilled desire for that baby. We could only assume she was crying because she was hungry. I say probably because we didn't know for sure why the baby was crying, we could only guess. Her parents must have guessed the same thing. Their first response was to find a bottle or something to stick in her mouth, at least that had worked before. It didn't work this time. Perhaps the baby was crying because she was hot or cold, or maybe the air pressure in the plane was causing her ears to hurt. The only thing we knew for sure was that the baby had a desire that had not yet been met. How many adults do you know who still cry, or whine, when they want something? (Been there, done that?)

The good news is that adult men and women actually can, and should, do something about their unfulfilled desires (assuming, of course, that those desires are moral). Adult men and women can usually discern an appropriate action to take to give themselves the best opportunity to fulfill their desires. The problem is that many people either put on internal noise-canceling headsets to squelch out the little voice compelling them to action, or they just delay taking the appropriate action to achieve their own desires. Either way is a recipe for failure. Others continue to cry and expect someone else to come to their aid and parentally fulfill their desire. That's why many people aren't champions. Champions are different; champions understand their desires and take appropriate action at the appropriate time to fulfill their desires. Champions think the right thoughts and are clear about their desires, and know what to do next.

Desire represents a void. Something is lacking. That *something* lacking most likely includes:

1) a clear understanding of what is missing;
2) a plan to meet that need
   (Chapter 6: *Champions Plan to Win*)
3) appropriate and decisive action
   (Chapter 7: *Implementation: Getting Past Getting Ready*)

So that raises the $10,000,000 question: "If the desire is morally good, and all three of the fulfillment qualifications listed above are met, then why at the end of the day is there still unfulfilled desire?" The answer is that there is untapped potential and the desire doesn't come as quickly as we would like. Sometimes we just need to drill a little deeper into our potential.

Desire is born and reborn daily in the sub-conscious, and it's in the sub-conscious that there is the understanding or knowledge of unrealized potential. In the sub-conscience, we know we can be or do better, and we are not satisfied until we do. Champions understand this and act upon it while pretenders only become more frustrated with life itself.

At Building Champions, we coach our clients to visualize the desired end-result of every discipline or project they undertake. The purpose is for them to fully consider the end from the beginning. Stephen Covey, in his landmark book *The 7 Habits of Highly Effective People*, called it *Habit 2: Begin with the End in Mind.* There is a desired end-result, and the best way to realize your goals is to remain focused on them from beginning to end. We call it vision; we recommend to our clients that they review their vision at the very least weekly. We will consider vision in greater detail in Chapter 5.

With a clear vision and thorough understanding of the desired end-result, one is poised to formulate a plan that includes appropriate action steps to be performed in a timely fashion. A plan without action is like a cloud without rain. A cloud with no rain doesn't water the seed that has been planted. Without rain, there is no fruit. Without appropriate and timely action, needs are left unsatisfied and goals are unfulfilled.

Remember, *desire* and *potential* are the key ingredients to success. They are the chief components of human achievement. The real difference among people (champions, players and pretenders alike) is what they do with those two ingredients. Most people have dreams (desire), and potential; champions do something constructive with theirs, while pretenders don't. Now let's consider the role potential plays in the making of a champion.

Champions Strive to Live Beyond Their Current Personal Best

You may have seen the ads on television that state: "A mind is a terrible thing to waste." I remember the first time I saw that ad; the point was that there were college students who couldn't attend school because of a lack of funds; and the intent was to raise money for a certain scholarship fund. Although I was only a child when I first saw that ad, I felt compelled to contribute (the problem was that I didn't have any funds to contribute... although my heart was in the right place). "A mind is a terrible thing to waste." What a profound statement!

Later in life, I realized a much deeper reality; potential is a terrible thing to waste. When wasted, it is more than just a mind that is wasted; it's opportunity, and talent, as well as the mind. Time is also wasted... the present, and to some extent the future.

Potential can be described in two ways:
1) Potential is energy that should be harnessed, and...
2) Potential is raw material that should be processed.

Think about it like this. You have the potential to be better, faster, stronger, smarter, and more successful than you are right now. The question is, "Why are you not?" We know that we can improve, yet too many people seem to be satisfied with the status quo and content with the knowledge that we "can be" some day. We can all be better than we are; yet most people do absolutely nothing about it. That's why most people aren't champions. Champions improve!

We have the potential to excel or fail... for the most part, excelling or failing comes down to choices. ***Potential is a gift. To harness and realize it is a choice.*** The choice to do nothing is in and of itself the choice to waste. The choice to ignore potential is the decision to resist change and to accept the status quo. The choice to accept the status quo is to choose failure. It's that simple.

There are actually two types of potential, "Known" and "Unknown". "Known" represents your current personal best in a specific endeavor. It's the highest level of performance that can be expected today. For example, if you lift weights while working out you may know what your "max" weight is for bench press. That would be the most weight you have ever lifted while lying on a bench. If you are training to run a marathon, you may know your personal best time for that particular distance. Those "Known" numbers represent the best you have ever done. But is your "Known" the best you can ever do? Probably not!

If "Known Potential" is a record that indicates your personal best performance to date, what is "Unknown"? "Unknown" represents what lies beyond your current "Known"... or what is beyond your experience. You have potential beyond your current best performance; your "Unknown" or "Unrealized Potential". It is that potential that constantly outdistances your current personal best. Champions are focused on not only matching their best performance to date, but to continually strive to improve their personal- best performance(s). Champions strive for new levels of "Known Potential"; they are always raising the bar. For many years it was commonly accepted that no human being could run a mile in less than four minutes. Roger Bannister proved that theory to be wrong. The amazing fact is that within a very short period of time, several other people broke that four-minute mile barrier. Prior to Roger Bannister, a 4 minute mile was an "Unknown Potential" mark that no one thought could be achieved. After he did it, the four-minute mile became "Known Potential" for the human race and quickly became "Known Potential" to one individual after another. It has been years since anything over a 4 minute mile qualified for even a bronze medal in the Olympics.

Champions recognize their current "Known Potential" as a temporary state. They are always focused on making their current "Known Potential" limits obsolete. Elite champions recognize world records as only the current "Known Potential" limits that can, and should be broken. Losers, on the other hand, accept the naysayers and are focused on the memory of how good it was to reach their current "Known Potential" limit, it becomes their badge of accomplishment; and they wear it proudly.

Everyone has good and bad days... and good and bad games. Your current "Known Potential" for playing today represents the best that you have ever done. The potential of that potential lies in the fact that as you continually improve, your best becomes better (your good days become better and your bad days are not as bad) – your good games become better and your bad games are not as bad – at that point, you have raised the bar of performance... you begin to realize the potential of your potential.

How much "Unknown Potential" do you have? Have you ever given it much thought? Just think about how many times that question comes up in a lifetime... a baby just starting to crawl: how fast will he or she be able to run? ...a young boy during little league tryouts: will he play major league baseball? ...a student making application to college: does he or she have what it takes to excel? ... Will they take advantage of that potential? Question after question, time after time, potential is evaluated by past performance and critical decisions are made based on that evaluation. Champions have learned that potential goes well beyond their current best performance... they consistently pursue their "Unknown Potential".

"Unknown Potential" is defined as that which exists in possibility or something that can be developed; therefore, that which can become actual. By definition, "Unknown Potential" is abstract; it only exists in possibility, it cannot actually be seen or physically measured. If that were possible, every one of us would know our absolute limits or ultimate personal "bests" in every area of life. As stated earlier, our "Unknown Potential" constantly outdistances our current performance. We can improve every day!

What a heavy thought! We can become better, stronger, faster, and smarter... whatever is necessary to improve our performance. That brings me to the next big question: "Is potential good or bad?" If we become complacent with our current personal "best" then our "Unknown Potential" only represents accomplishments that could have been but never were realized. However, if we approach our current "best" in any endeavor as a springboard or launching pad to strive for improvement, then potential is good. To better understand that statement we must first understand what I call the ***Dichotomy of Potential.***

<u>Champions Understand the Dichotomy of Potential</u>
The Pebble & the Apple Seed

Imagine holding an apple seed in one hand and a pebble in the other. The pebble is living up to its full potential. There is no "Unknown Potential" for the pebble. On its own, the pebble will never grow into a rock, a rock will never grow into a boulder, and a boulder will never grow into a mountain. How is the apple seed different? When you hold an apple seed in your hand, you are "potentially" holding more than just one small apple seed in the palm of your hand. You are "potentially" holding a fruit bearing apple tree; apples that can be baked in an apple pie with melting ice cream streaming down those baked apples (you get the picture). The seeds in that apple potentially can become an apple orchard; an orchard with hundreds of seed bearing apple trees. Consider the "Unknown Potential" of one little apple seed! Better yet, just think about the "Unknown Potential" inside of you! How much fruit do you have the potential to bear?

The Dichotomy of Potential reveals that, along with the lack of potential to grow into anything more, the pebble lacks the potential to disappoint you. It is living up to your full expectations. The apple seed, however, with all of its potential to become a perpetual apple orchard, possesses an equal amount of potential to disappoint you. The virtue of having potential that raises expectations carries with it an equal amount of potential to disappoint; thus raising again the question: "Is potential good or bad?" I believe the answer to that question lies in whether appropriate action is taken at the appropriate time to pursue the fulfillment of potential rather than allow it to remain dormant.

<u>Appropriate Action + Appropriate Timing =
Realized Potential</u> (Known and Unknown)

The best way I can relate this concept is by sharing with you a story about a guy we will call J.R. Potential. I first met J.R. several years ago when we were working for the same organization. Our career paths crossed when I was named as manager (I prefer the term leader) responsible for three areas of our organization, one of which was J.R. Potential's area. He was in a critical position with our organization because his area was responsible for the final stage in the process of prepping our product for the customer. He was the last person to actually see our product before it was delivered to the customer.

I vividly recall the day I took the reigns of my new areas of responsibility. As you might imagine, there was a line of people wanting to offer me advice and insight as to how I should lead. There was profitable advice, and there were suggestions that I simply needed to ignore. One piece of advice, however, was one that was repeated to me over and over again. This advice intrigued me the most. That advice was to ignore J.R.'s area and let that "big dog" continue to sleep on the porch, as we would say in the South. (It simply means that a sleeping dog won't bite; but if you wake him up, you could be in trouble.) I was told that he had potential, and that potential was the ability to cause trouble; therefore, it would be in my best interest to leave well enough alone and concentrate on the other two areas of my new responsibility.

The people who know me well know that I just couldn't stay away. Curiosity may have killed the cat, but there was no way I was going to leave well enough alone, especially when there were improvements needed in J.R.'s area. One of the first things I did was to visit him.

I wish I could tell you that when I got there I found that my "advisors" were wrong about him. When I arrived in his area I found, not only everything I heard about him to be true—it was worse! The picture painted for me concerning him omitted a host of negative attributes. I found myself involved in one very serious situation. I had walked up the stairs of the porch, marched right up to that sleeping dog and kicked it with all I had in me. Now what will I do? Was this a career-killing lack of judgment on my part to ignore the advice to stay away? There was no walking away. At this point it really didn't matter, I was there and I was committed to success.

He was a complainer and took every opportunity to let any one that would listen hear all about how bad the company was, how bad the leaders were, and he would rave about how few resources he was given to operate his area. I made the decision that I was going to listen to what I didn't want to hear, and see what I didn't want to see, so that I might understand what no one else had taken the time to understand. In my heart I felt that he was an apple seed, not a pebble. I chose to believe that others before me were so negative about him because they were only seeing the negative or flip side of his potential... the same potential that the apple seed had to disappoint.

As time went by, and as I listened to what he had to say, I realized that, in his heart, all he really wanted was for his area to be one of, if not the best, in the organization. He was frustrated because no one would listen to him or respond to his requests. He had been on a slippery slope and was going downhill fast. This stemmed from the fact that no one would listen to what he had to say. He had been brushed aside and put on the back burner until he became bitter and resistant to the leadership of that organization. The good news was that things were about to change.

The more time I invested in listening to him, the more I realized what was beneath the surface, behind the calloused outside that everyone else saw. One of the most important things we practice as coaches at Building Champions is called "Active Listening", listening which is intent on fully understanding what the other person is trying to say. By doing this, I found that he had a heart of gold, and some awesome ideas concerning his area. It didn't take long for him to start to open up to me and share those ideas. Although some of his ideas, at that time, were beyond consideration, there were those that merited future study, and there were those that we could implement immediately. The approach I took was simple.

The first issues we tackled were those that we could implement immediately without approval from anyone else. Soon the mutual trust he and I had developed allowed me to explain to him why we had to implement some of his ideas before others and why some just needed to be tabled. Because of our mutual trust, he knew that I would be candid with him and he believed that I was looking out for his best interest along with the best interest of the organization.

Things started to change and noticeable improvements were made. Before long others started to see the changes in his department along with the obvious changes in his attitude. His area soon became a showplace for our organization. In fact, there were many requests to allow our customers to tour his area. His domain had become a source of pride for the entire organization. The spotlight was tilted in my direction because of the sweeping changes and improvements that had been made. Although the attention was pleasing, I knew that all I had done was to recognize that J.R. had "Unknown Potential". His previous personal best wasn't nearly as good as what he and his area had become. My role had been as a facilitator to help him realize his potential.

Subsequently, I was given the opportunity to showcase what I had accomplished as the leader of that area. Executives flew in from around the world for a meeting where various leaders could exchange information and relate the successes they had achieved in their specific areas of responsibility. Although it would have been easy to take center stage and take the credit, I decided to take a different approach.

I invited J.R. to actually take my place and give the presentation himself! Once again I had to overcome all of the naysayers who told me that I was making a big mistake by letting him have the spotlight, but I did it anyway.

At first he was nervous and didn't want to be a presenter, but I convinced him that since he was the source of the ideas and was also the chief implementer that he should be the one to tell the story. I told him that I would help him create his presentation and that I would be present when he gave it. When that day came, the presentation was ready, he was polished in his delivery, and I sat on the sidelines and clicked the mouse as he presented the slides. What happened during that presentation totally amazed not only me, but everyone in the room.

You recall that even before we started preparation of the presentation and his delivery, I was questioned by some executives. They asked if I thought it was a good idea to allow him to take center stage. After all, in their eyes, it was my area and I was being given the opportunity to "look good" to our executive team. I was also asked if I was the least bit concerned about what he would say when given the chance to speak to these executives. At one point, I was even cautioned that, by allowing him to give the presentation, I was taking a chance with the advancement of my own career.

Nevertheless, I was convinced that allowing J.R. to "strut his stuff" was the right thing to do. My parents had taught me that if I would always do what is right, I could rest in the fact that things would work out for the best. What happened in that room that day was truly amazing.

As he gave the presentation, and as I sat at a side table clicking the mouse for him, I noticed something strange. The executives in attendance were doing three things: 1) watching and listening to him; 2) taking notes and, 3) looking at me with glances of amazement. By the end of the presentation, they had additional questions for J.R. and me; afterwards we were both congratulated for the major improvements that had occurred in that area. Even the naysayers realized that by taking the spotlight off me and allowing it to be on him, I had actually intensified the light that was shining on me. As it turned out, this was a huge win-win for me, for J.R., and for our organization as a whole! The most incredible segment of the J.R. story, however, was yet to come.

After I had moved on in my career path to another organization, he continued to grow and make positive things happen in his area of responsibility. Several years later I saw him again, and with a huge smile on his face he told me that things were going very well for him. In fact, he told me that he had been offered several higher level leadership positions within the company over the years. When I asked him what he was doing, he just smiled again and said he was doing the same thing he was doing when I left. He said he was doing what he loved to do. He is a champion and he is pursuing his "Unknown Potential" in his area of responsibility!

The point here is not some great leadership principle I learned while working on my MBA. It is simply that J.R. (like most of us) had Potential—the potential to improve and to live like a champion every day, because every day is Game Day! All I did was to recognize that potential and then set the table for his success. His "Known Potential" was consistently realized, and continues to be realized as he pursues his "Unknown Potential". That's what happens when the appropriate action is taken at the appropriate time. So now, what was once "Unknown Potential" has now become his "Known Potential" and the new "Unknown Potential" is his goal. It's really that simple.

What holds you back?

Are you realizing your full "Known Potential" and chasing your "Unknown Potential" like a true champion? If not, what is holding you back? Too many times it's easier to blame someone else (like J.R. had once done) than to look inside and take responsibility for our own development. I am convinced that at times, as in the case of J.R., we all may need a nudge. That nudge could come from an accountability partner, which is part of our coaching program at Building Champions. The fact is that champions take responsibility for the achievement of their desired levels of success. The first step in that direction is to realize what is holding you back.

So what is it that holds you back? Is it a lack of knowledge? ...lack of skill? ... the fear of failure? ...or maybe fear of success? Most obstacles that hold us back can be overcome, but only if they have been recognized. Once the barrier or barriers to success are recognized, actionable steps can be taken to effectively overcome whatever it is that stands in your way. It may mean that you find yourself stumbling and falling over and over again until you get it right; that's ok as long as you are consistently learning and improving. In his book *Failing Forward*, John Maxwell discusses the point that failing can be good if we learn from our failures. Champions learn from their failures, get up, and win. Some people don't fail because they don't try... those people aren't champions.

Champions Play – Pretenders Stay at Bay

Sometimes potential is unclear. Sometimes your current personal best is undetermined because you haven't *gotten off the bench*. At times, there isn't even a historical best to be referenced because there is no history of attempt. This can possibly be attributed to a lack of desire. There is no real success if potential is not married to desire. To illustrate: Union University is a well-respected private school in Jackson, TN. On any given day you can walk around campus and see students wearing red tee shirts stating:

Union University Football
Undefeated Since 1963

Wow! What a run! Undefeated since 1963? Who else can boast of such a record? Well, the truth is that several schools can boast of such a record; schools like Union that don't have a football team, and haven't had one since 1963. Just the other day, my son came home from his school sporting a pullover with the message: "Lee Football... Undefeated since 1918". It's not that they had a longer winning streak than Union... they just have never had a football team. The fact is that Union University, and Lee University, have made the conscience decision not to have a football team because after weighing the options and considering the pros and cons, there was no desire. So, it's easy to go undefeated if you don't participate in the game. The shirts could just as easily have read: *"Without a Win Since (whatever year)!"* because we haven't played.

That's not the case with the Union University Lady Bulldogs basketball team. Under the direction of Head Coach Mark Campbell, Union's Lady Bulldogs won back-to-back NAIA National Championships in 2005 and 2006. An interesting, and important fact is that they were not undefeated in either of those two years. In fact, at one point late in the 2006 season they had lost seven games in a row over the past two years to nearby rival Freed - Hardeman Lady Lions. That's right. They had won one national championship and were well on their way to winning another, but had lost to another team within thirty miles of their campus seven times in a row! The desire and potential tandem does not promise anything other than, if acted upon, the opportunity to win at life, business, sports, or whatever you pour yourself into. Champions realize that there comes a time to stop practicing at life... the clock is already running.

Anytime you act upon your desire and call upon your potential, you are putting yourself at risk. Remember that the apple seed has as much opportunity to disappoint as it does to fulfill promise, as does action taken on desire and potential. The guarantee is that if you don't act upon your desire and call upon your potential, you will never win. So the question becomes: How do I appropriately act upon my desire and attempt to fulfill my potential in a timely fashion? The answer(s) to the question(s) will become clear as you continue to read.

The Way Out

How do I evaluate my game? How do I start? Those are great questions, and the fact that you continue to read indicates that you have something inside of you that drives you to be a champion. The way up begins with recognizing and consistently acting on the potential you already possess. What is your past personal best performance? – Or – What do you believe it to be? Why aren't you achieving it every day? What are the obstacles to consistently achieving your "Known Potential" and pursuing your "Unknown Potential" every day? What are the gaps between your average daily performance and your current personal best? How can those gaps be closed? Once these questions are answered and appropriate and timely action is taken, you will begin to see that what once was your personal best could become the norm. At that point you will be on the champion's road to chasing a new personal-best! You will take this fresh understanding of the Dichotomy of Potential and live beyond your current personal-bests like a true champion never worrying about being an unfruitful apple seed! Complete the Power Plays at the end of this chapter and you will see new opportunities to move in the direction of the achievement of your goals. The way up will continue with discovering your purpose; we will consider that in Chapter Three. First, complete the Power Plays for Chapter Two… Then read on champion!

Power Plays – Chapter 2

- List 2-3 areas specific to your life and 2-3 areas specific to your career that you know you have the potential to perform better than you've ever performed before.

- What is holding you back? Honestly assess your situation and clearly define, in your opinion, the reason you believe you have not enjoyed the level of success you should have reached by now in life and business.

- Determine, and document the action(s) that you need to take in order to open the door of opportunity to find those greater levels of success. Commit to make those changes. (How does this compare to your response to the Power Plays in Chapter 1?)

- Read *Failing Forward* by John Maxwell

- Read *The Traveler's Gift* by Andy Andrews

CHAPTER 3

From a Life Sentence to a Life on Purpose

―᎗᎗᎗――

On January 25, 1975, 18-year-old Maury Davis, in a drug-altered state of confusion, entered a home in Irving, Texas. The motive was burglary, the end-result... murder. When he walked out of that house that fateful day, a human being was dead and Maury Davis was soon to be a wanted man. In one split second, although he was still a free man on the outside, chains of bondage on the inside immediately incarcerated him. There was no way to *unlive* the previous ten minutes. In one brief moment, his future became influenced by a violent, impulsive action. It was that day in which the choices of his past culminated with present actions to forever change his future. It was Game Day for Maury Davis.

Murder was a crime he couldn't run from... but he tried. Later that day, after spending some time with his girl-friend, he brought her back home to Stafford Street in Irving. Moments after they went inside, he passed out on the couch; probably due to the heavy use of drugs and alcohol he had used to escape the reality of what he had done. He awakened at 6AM the next morning and got in his car parked in her driveway. It was then that Maury realized he had actually spent the night there in her house. When he backed out of the driveway and started to drive back to his apartment, he passed the detectives that were coming to arrest him. Their investigation had led them to her house. The emotional chains that had him bound on the inside were about to be joined by physical shackles on the outside.

His first inclination was to run, and so a high-speed chase began. That bolt to maintain his external freedom lasted 15-20 minutes, involving several patrol cars. He swerved all over the road and even drove through neighborhood yards trying to get away... trying to remain free (on the outside). At speeds up to 80 mph, it was a perilous situation for him as well as the officers giving chase. Innocent by-standers at that time of the morning were in grave danger. Something had to be done. One policeman made the decision to end the chase by ramming Maury's car into a tree. Almost instantly, after his car slammed into the tree, he looked up and saw another officer laying on the hood of his car with a shotgun against the windshield pointed directly into his face. All he could hear was that policeman shouting, "Don't move! Don't move!" He was surrounded with nowhere to go.

The chase had ended, but the long road to finding purpose and complete freedom had just begun! His focus now shifted to his internal struggles... Externally, there was no place left to run. The destiny of his external life was going to be dictated by a decision made by a jury and the judge that would sentence him. Maury sensed that he still had some control over the destiny of his life, and that control rested on his personal decisions and actions from that day forward. It was time for him to discover and then to start taking action to live a life dedicated to the fulfillment of what he was born to do. The quest for purpose is primarily an inside job.

Maury, though incarcerated, knew he could still exercise his freedom to think, dream and to believe.

The trial lasted one week. Eleven of the jurors voted to give him a life sentence (which wasn't bad considering the state in which he committed the crime)... but one juror, Don McDaniel, commented that God's justice always has mercy. The decision of that one man to plead the cause of mercy not only affected Maury's life, but also the life of his family, and thousands of people Maury was yet to meet. Even with this call for mercy, he was still a convicted man waiting to be sentenced. Armed with the jury's decision, the judge sentenced Maury Davis to 20 years with the Texas State Department of Corrections.

Seated on a cold steel bench, with a leather belt around his waist connected to his chained hands, shackled to another inmate, Maury began the 6.5-hour Texas Department of Corrections bus ride to his new home away from home. My friend Maury said it was one of the most difficult days of his life because he knew that at the end of that journey, he would be in prison for a long time. The emotions he experienced were unimaginable.

As I am writing this chapter, I have just returned from a family vacation where I was severely sunburned because of a bad decision on my part not to wear sun block. I have blisters on my back from the sunburn and I am in such pain, it hurts to even think about putting on a shirt. Just as Maury didn't leave his apartment the morning of January 25, 1975, with intentions of killing another person, I didn't go on vacation with the intention of being severely burned. Although I knew better, I didn't do what I needed to do (put on sun block) until it was too late. It was a cool and cloudy day; I was comfortable, and preoccupied. How many times do we by-pass doing what we know we should do, or do what we know we shouldn't do, only to pay dearly for it later? Philosopher Jim Rohn states that the things we know we should do, and can do, but don't do represent a formula for disaster. He also said the things that are easy to do are also easy not to do… it was easy for me to put sun block on that day… it was also easy not to. Fortunately, I will be "released" from this confining pain in a couple of days. Maury was looking at 20 years in a Texas prison.

He was assigned to the Texas State Department of Corrections - Ferguson Unit just off Texas state road 247. The Ferguson unit covers thousands of acres of cattle and farmland. Along the road leading up to the unit is a little community where the guards and their families live. While soaking in the scenery, Maury knew this could virtually be the last glimpse of freedom he would see for years. Ferguson Unit is a maximum-security prison. Tall barbed wire fences surround the facility, with searchlights and heavily armed guards in towers around the prison. But nestled behind the barbed wire, in the midst of the multiple cell buildings, is a little chapel where Maury would attend his first church service— a place where he would grow into a deeper understanding of, and passion for his meaning in life.

It was in prison that he learned that freedom is one of the greatest gifts of opportunity God has given to us: freedom to do, freedom to be, and freedom to become. He found that he could have unbelievable freedom on the *inside* even while his physical body was imprisoned. (Victor Frankl in his highly acclaimed book, *Man's Search for Meaning,* beautifully expresses the triumph of the spirit in the face of oppression and physical imprisonment.)

There was nothing, at this point, Maury could do about the victim of his crime. His remorse was (and still is) great. If there were only some way to bring this person back to life – but there isn't. What's done is done, whether it be the result of specific action we have taken, or in some cases the lack of action. There is no way for Maury to take back, or "unlive" his actions. His only choice was to ask for forgiveness and move on. He did that, but physically he was still a long-term guest of the state of Texas.

However, it was in prison that Maury made the decision that never again would he surrender his freedom. In an effort to solidify this decision, Maury memorized a verse of Scripture: "It is for freedom that Christ has set us free. Stand firm, then, and do not let yourselves be burdened again by a yoke of slavery." (Galatians 5:1 NIV) It was there that Maury Davis began to discover, and then take decisive action to fully live out his purpose in life. What a place to start on the journey to complete and lasting freedom! You too can begin that journey to discover your purpose and live a life of freedom today.

In a five-by-nine cell made of concrete blocks and cold steel bars, Maury had experienced the loneliness that no human ever intends to experience... a pervasive loneliness in the midst of four to five thousand other men experiencing similar emotions. Loneliness in an environment where a person has no privacy, even to use the restroom... loneliness in a place where his toilet was only two feet from the bunk beds shared by him and his cell mate. Maury was lonely, but not alone. He was beginning to experience unbelievable freedom on the inside.

Maury said that the only thing he had to console him, other than a handful of prisoners experiencing this same internal freedom, was a Bible. During the days leading up to his crime, he didn't really know who he was or where he was going. He was living from drink to drink and high to high. He felt no real meaning in life. Maury's description of his life makes me think of the term "strung out" which is a term used to describe people in a state of drug-induced semi-consciousness. Maury's life, at the time of his crime, was strung out. He was living in a world where he did anything he wanted, and yet he didn't really want to do what he did. He was his own worst enemy, alive in a world where he was only focused on feeding his desires without ever feeling fulfilled. He was looking for something that was there all along; he was just looking in the wrong places.

Maury said that when a person is imprisoned, hours seem like days, days seem like weeks, and weeks seem like months until time becomes blurred. Day after day, week after week, month after month, time passed by ever so slowly for Maury. There were times when he said he didn't know if he could live any longer... but he did... and as he did, his purpose became clear. That little Bible, along with some special inmate friends that he said God placed in his life, gave him hope. Maury explains it as a hope that could not be extinguished.

How many of us are locked in our own prisons, desiring to be free but still chained to whatever put us there? How many of us are chained by our own devices, living our days, weeks and months "strung out" with only a fading flame of hope that once burned strong? Hope is the spark that ignites the passion for purpose. Hope can be an anchor for the soul, but that anchor will only hold firm if it is supported by intentional action directed toward the resolution of living with meaning. We find that faith is being sure of what we hope for and that faith without works is dead. Without works, or positive directed action, there is no true hope—only wishful thinking.

Maury found hope in his purpose and anchored that hope with the limited action he could take while in prison. After eight and a half years he was released, free to pursue that hope with unfettered potential. Fresh out of prison, Maury started working in, a most unlikely place, a church. He had just been released from prison for murder. Who would want to hire him? Someone did, he was hired to clean toilets. That's right, Maury Davis had desire and potential, and while cleaning the church toilets, he was in the process of discovering his ultimate direction. The fact is that he was actually living his life to the best of his ability and opportunity at that time, being the best toilet cleaner he could be. That's all any of us could ever hope to do: live every day like a champion, doing the best we can with what we currently have, because every day is Game Day!

Maury says that today, his chief aim in life is to serve God by making a positive difference in the lives of others. He had the opportunity to do that by offering his services in the area of housekeeping at Calvary Temple in Irving. The rest, as they say, is history. After serving the eight and a half years in the Texas Corrections System, Maury served five years on staff at Calvary Temple, and then as a full time evangelist traveling across the United States preaching at churches, youth camps and Bible schools, as well as speaking to teens in public schools. In 1991 he was offered the position of senior pastor of the 250-member Cornerstone Church in Madison, Tennessee. Today, Cornerstone has over 2,000 members and donates over a million dollars a year to positively impact other people around the world. Maury Davis is living like a champion... Maury Davis lives with purpose!

You too can discover meaning and begin to live like a champion every day knowing that every day is Game Day. If that's what you want, let's begin by observing the Three Principles of Purpose.

Finding Purpose at the Intersection of Desire and Potential

Like Maury Davis (before he found purpose) too many people are wasting precious time, serving a self-inflicted life sentence when they should be living like champions every day. One of the best-selling books ever written is Rick Warren's *The Purpose Driven Life*. In that book, Rick begins with, what may at first seem to be a very strange statement for a book on purpose. His first words are: "It's not about you." He couldn't have opened with better words! The reason so many people are leading a humdrum life is because they are too focused on their own immediate desires. Your purpose, however, is so much bigger than just you and your never fully satisfied daily cravings! It's when you focus only on yourself that you are limited to one- dimensional thinking (thinking about you alone). One-dimensional thinking only allows you to focus on the fulfillment of a small piece of who you were created to be. When you realize that many of your actions affect those around you either positively or negatively, you will begin to see the power and potential of your life in multiple dimensions. You begin to realize that everything done (or not done) by those around you really does affect you. Therefore, helping others ultimately helps you! At some point in the discovery process you will have the epiphany that your purpose really isn't just about you... and yet, at the same time, it is all about you!

So what is your purpose? Although much has been written about it, too many people never seem to recognize, or even attempt to live according to their purpose. Far too many people wander aimlessly through life, almost limping from one day to the next with no idea of the potential they have to impact the world around them in a positive way. Is that you or someone you know? It doesn't have to be! You can (and should) discover your purpose... and live according to it every day because every day is Game Day!

The Hiding Place of Purpose: Your Heart

There is no way an outsider, like me, can prove to you that you have a purpose... it's an inside job. However, no one can escape the fact that they have purpose. It's pre-wired in our DNA. If your reason for being on this earth seems to be hidden… it's undoubtedly hidden inside of you. However, I don't believe it is *hidden* from you, but rather, for whatever reason, *covered* by you. The good news is that it can be discovered (or in some cases re-discovered). Some people allow their purpose to be covered because they are not willing to put forth the effort to fulfill it; so it's just easier to allow it to lie dormant. These people are usually the most miserable of all because they have a sense of what they can accomplish, but they postpone action for a multitude of reasons, until they are lost in a world of "would haves", "could haves", and "should haves". No one is given a purpose he or she cannot fulfill. If that were true, there would be no "purpose" for purpose.

Along this journey we call life, there are clues that help us discover our purpose. Consider this: *"Purpose begins to come into focus at the point where desire intersects with potential."* What a statement! You already know your areas of interest (those things that grab your attention and captivate you). You already know what you are good at doing (or at least what you could be good at doing if you only apply yourself to the discipline of improvement). Now all you have to do to begin the discovery process is to connect the dots. When you do, you will be surprised at how clear your mission on this planet can be. That's when you can really start living on purpose— the only way to live a fulfilled life.

Connecting the dots is only the beginning of the discovery process; "purpose begins to come into focus at the point where desire (your areas of interest) intersects with potential (what you are… or could be good at doing). Certainly, everything I want to do and have the potential to do is not directly connected to my purpose. That thought could get me in a lot of trouble. However, connecting those dots is the starting point. To better understand this process of discovering your purpose, let's look at three very specific principles that you must believe and accept as truth in order to discover your purpose and start living your life with meaning.

The 3 Principles of Purpose

Purpose Principle #1
Everyone has a purpose.

Purpose Principle #2
Everyone can, and should, know their purpose.

Purpose Principle #3
Everyone can, and should, be taking action to fulfill their purpose every day.

Considering the question about the chicken and the egg, in the case of these three principles, the egg (your purpose and potential) definitely comes before the chicken (living on purpose every day). In this instance it is permissible to count your chickens before they hatch…it's just up to you to make sure they do hatch.

First of all, notice the definitive tense (or nature) of <u>Purpose Principle #1</u>:
"Everyone **has** a purpose."
… and the indefinite nature of <u>Purpose Principle #2</u>:
"Everyone **can, and should**, know their purpose
…and, <u>Purpose Principle #3</u>:
"Everyone **can, and should**, take action to fulfill his or her purpose."

Purpose Principle 1

We have a purpose. I have never met a person who truly believed that he/she had absolutely no purpose at all. At least at one time in our lives, all of us have felt special. That special feeling comes from the sense that we have a connection with the world around us, including the people around us. It's within this connection that we may discover meaning. Each of us, at one time or another, has been interested in something that we know has the potential to deliver good results for others and ourselves. That comes from the fact that we have purpose. Remember, our desire for purpose is pre-wired in our DNA.

Purpose Principles 2 & 3

The indefinite nature of Principles 2 & 3 which includes the words *can* and *should* offers the first clues as to why many people don't know or live according to their purpose. These are the eggs that don't or won't hatch. In other words, we can all know and fulfill our purpose (make the eggs hatch)... but many *don't*, they *should*, but *won't* attempt to discover and take action to fulfill their purpose. There are so many people who either haven't discovered this, or don't take action to fulfill it. The underlying premise is that it's all up to you to make this discovery (the eggs that should hatch), and then take positive and definite action toward fulfillment (making the eggs hatch).

The rest of this chapter is dedicated to two types of people:
1) those who want to move from not knowing their purposes to being clear about them, and
2) those who already know their purposes and want to move from the recognition to fulfillment stage.

Purpose Principle 2

Everyone can, and should, know their purpose.
Discovering purpose is not as difficult as some may think.
Why is it so challenging to discover why we exist? There are
two schools of thought: 1) many people are apathetic and
choose not to look for it, and 2) others are afraid of failure
(or maybe even success). It's through the discovery process
that we learn to appreciate the value and uniqueness of our
purpose. To some, that is a scary thought... the thought that
if I know my purpose and don't fulfill it, I am a failure.

Although there is no prescribed method or course to
discovering your purpose, the following Power Play offers a
simple tool to get you started on the journey.

Discovering Your Purpose: The First Step

A.) List 3-5 things in life that draw your attention or
captivate your imagination? Consider the following
questions:

-What were your favorite (or easiest) subjects
in school?

- What do you daydream about most?

-If money were no object, how would you
invest your time each day?

-What do you really enjoy doing?

B.) List 3-5 things that you are either already good at
doing, or know you could be good at doing if you
apply yourself.

C.) Connect the dots: Use any combination of lists A
& B to describe a situation or time when you were
combining any item(s) on list "A" with any item(s)

on list "B" that ultimately benefited you and / or others around you. This could also include a time when an item or items in list "A" was not, but could have been combined with any item or items in list "B" to benefit yourself and / or those around you. Record those responses in list "C".

List A	List B	List C
_____	_____	_____
_____	_____	_____
_____	_____	_____
_____	_____	_____

Bingo! It's in List "C" that you find the point(s) where desire intersects with potential to create opportunity for you to have a positive impact on your own life and on those around you. This is the point or points where your purpose begins to come into focus. Using this new knowledge you can begin to write your own mission or purpose statement.

Obviously there is no one exercise or set of questions that will reveal your overall purpose in life. The process of discovery takes time and effort, but it's well worth the journey. The good news is that you are already further down that road of discovery than the vast majority of people around you— people who are just letting the clocks of their lives tick away day in and day out, not having a clue as to why in the world they are on this planet.

-www.gamedaychampions.com   is a great place to find resources that will help you continue the discovery process.

Now that you are on your way, let's go ahead and look at Purpose Principle 3 so that once you discover your purpose, you'll be on the right path to do what you need to do.

Purpose Principle 3

The third principle states that: "We can, and should, be taking daily action to fulfill our purposes." Taking appropriate action in your life is critical to your success. You are the only one who can take the necessary action in this area. As author and speaker Jim Rohn once said: "No one can do your push-ups for you... you have to do them yourself."

Potential is powerful...but only if we exercise it. As we learned in Chapter 2, the "Dichotomy of Potential" tells us that we are more like the apple seed than the pebble in respect to potential but, with that potential comes an equal amount of opportunity for disappointment. Just as the pebble is living up to its full potential and will never experience disappointment, the apple seed, with all of its potential, has a 50/50 chance of being either fruitful or barren. Although potential, with its high expectations, is good, be assured that there is also risk involved. Risk requires the development of courage.

In the next chapter you will have the opportunity to read about two incredible men who have lived courageously on purpose. You will learn that courage is both fueled and directed by what you have just discovered.

Complete the Power Play for this chapter and then read Chapter 4 to discover the courage you need to continue this journey of championship living.

Power Plays – Chapter 3

- Write a sentence or two about what it is that is driving you to a purpose filled life.

- Make a list of the 5 things you would do if time and money were no object. Dream big.

- Principle 1: Describe a time in your life that you felt fulfilled. Identify and write the reason or reasons why this gave you the sense of fulfillment.

- Read *The On-Purpose Person* by Kevin McCarthy

- Read *The Purpose Driven Life* by Rick Warren

- Principle 2: Review your responses in this section of the chapter

- Read *Building Your Company's Vision* article from the Harvard Business Review written by Jim Collins and Jerry Porras – September – October 1996 – Reprint #96501

- Using the format given in the "Core Purpose" section of that article, write your own Purpose Statement

- Principle 3: What are the daily actions that you need to take to live according to your stated purpose? Use the Keep – Start – Stop process to help you think deeper in this area. What are you currently doing that you need to KEEP doing? What are you not currently doing that you need to START doing? Finally, what are you currently doing that you can, or should, STOP doing?

CHAPTER 4

Champions Exhibit Courage Every Day
Courage is a Choice Driven by Purpose

———

I t's on the battlefield that courage is exhibited. In fact, courage can only be recognized in the midst of battle. Without battle there is no basis for courage. Battles come in all shapes and sizes and are ever present, lurking at the gateways of our lives. We never know, however, when one of those battles will either be ushered in by ceremonial splendor like a thunderstorm brewing on the horizon in the Deep South in early spring, or just quietly slither onto the stage of our lives like an undetected cancer. The reality is that every day we live on this earth we are faced with battles and opportunities to exhibit courage. Some battles just grab our attention and require more courage than others.

Whether in the heat of an attention grabbing battle or in the mundane moments of every day life, courage can and should be evident. Most people think of courage as a flash of bravery and significance like lightning and thunder. While that is true, enduring courage may be observed in every day longsuffering and endurance. *Everyday courage* is realized when someone stands boldly in the gap between a truth which demands action and the fallacy of false hope coupled with no action. This courage stands firm in the face of fear and criticism until the battle is won, whether the battle is large or small.

One battle that grabbed our collective attention and awakened our national consciousness reared its' ugly head on 9/11/2001... the battle with global terrorism. Until that day, most of us didn't recognize terrorism as a global issue because it appeared that we, in this country, were exempt. On the morning of that dreadful day, the world, as we knew it, changed... the unthinkable happened. We were attacked on our own soil by terrorists using American commercial passenger planes as missiles. That day the proverbial line was drawn in the sand and we, as a nation, had to either step up to the plate and choose the actionable path of courage, or live with fear, in the fallacy of false hope that nothing like this would ever happen again. That day, President George W. Bush stood toe to toe with the tyranny of terror, looked directly into the television camera and proclaimed, *"Terrorist attacks can shake the foundations of our biggest buildings, but they cannot touch the foundation of America. These acts shatter steel, but they cannot dent the steel of American resolve... Make no mistake: The United States will hunt down and punish those responsible for these cowardly acts... The resolve of our great nation is being tested. But make no mistake: We will show the world that we will pass this test. God Bless America."* It was evident that the courage of our leader was clear and his message concise.

Let's contrast that with lack of courage. Although the lack of courage may not, at times, be as evident, it is in fact, much more abundant. Those who lack courage can turn their heads, look the other way, and hide for a period of time; but in the end, there is always shame and disgrace. Consider this poem written by my son at age 15. It was published in the *Anthology of Poetry by Young Americans – 2002 Edition*.

<u>A Knight's Fear</u>
By
Adam Enochs

I never was an honored man,
I was disowned within the land.
My father's sword upon my side,
He gave it to me the day he died.
I worked for years to become a knight,
But not one evildoer did I smite.
Every time the king sent me out,
I ran and hid with fear and doubt.
I wanted to help in the wars,
But I stayed behind the safety of my doors.
The people laughed from time to time,
I felt like I had committed an awful crime.
I watched my father fight and die,
When I ran toward him as I cried.
Ever since then I've been afraid to fight,
So soon I will feel the pain of death's bite.
I am now on the battlefield,
But my sword I will not wield.
Even as the arrows fly,
I will not fight even if I die.
My blood now pours out like a river,
Into God's hands my life is delivered.

Oh, the wisdom in the words of a 15-year-old boy! Have you seen this knight? Do you know this knight? Is it you? If it is you, can you change? Yes! You can become a knight of courage, but it's up to you. Let's take a closer look...

"I never was an honored man.
I was disowned within the land..."

What does it mean to be an honored man or woman? The word honor has to do with the act or fact of being true to what is right. It is great respect given because of worth, noble deeds, and high rank. It can be exemplified in a good name, or reputation to uphold. It has been said that honor is given or bestowed. Yet, honor must first be *earned* before it is ever *given.* In the biblical book of Proverbs, King Solomon, the wisest man who ever lived put it this way: "Like tying a stone in a sling is the giving of honor to a fool." (NIV) Who would tie a stone in a sling? In today's vernacular, it would be like super gluing an arrow to the bowstring. Why should honor ever be given to a fool? Although the knight in our poem had become a knight by title, he was not given honor; in fact, he was even disowned within the land.

Why was this knight never honored? Why was he disowned within the land? After all, he was a knight! By definition, a knight was a man in the Middle Ages who was given a military rank of honor after serving as a page and squire: knights were expected to be gallant and brave. This knight had the rank of military honor bestowed upon him because he had gone through the training of first being a page, then a squire. He had earned the right to be called a knight; only in battle could he earn the right to be an honored knight. In the Middle Ages, a page was a boy in training to become a knight. A squire was a young man who attended a knight. Perhaps it was on the final day of serving as a squire, while attending to a knight, that this young man saw his dad die in battle.

Training to become a knight and actually being an honored man as a knight of noble service are two entirely different things. As we see in the poem, it was his lack of courage that not only cost him honor in the land, but also cost him his life. He died in midst of his fear... because of his fear. He lacked courage.

During the NFL playoffs of the 2003/2004 season the St. Louis Rams played the Carolina Panthers in St. Louis. The game had gone back and forth with the lead changing hands several times. In the fourth quarter, with 30 seconds to go in the game, the Rams had the ball within reasonable striking distance of the goal line... plenty of time to run at least two plays, one attempt to get into the end zone for the win, and one to kick a game tying field goal. For whatever reason, the coach decided to take the ball out of the hands of one of the most potent offenses in the NFL and run the clock down to just enough time to kick the tying field goal. The Rams went into overtime only to lose to the Panthers who went on to play in one of the most exciting Super Bowl games in the history of the NFL... while the Rams watched. What was the difference? Although we will never know what would have happened had the Rams utilized the time they had to run that one additional play to attempt to win the game, we do know that by not going for it they eventually lost. It has been said that, "You miss 100% of the shots you do not take." They didn't take the shot.

Many wanted to blame the coach. Some called for his replacement— all due to a 30-second decision to play it safe. The coach momentarily succumbed to the same emotion as our un-honored and disowned knight, fear. I believe that this coach was one of the best in the NFL. It was only one decision, but a costly one for the Rams. Sometimes you only have seconds to choose the path of courage.

Does fear grip your heart in a way that paralyzes your ability to choose the path of courage and live like a champion? Do you freeze up when given an opportunity, simply because there is an element of risk involved? There is good news and bad news! The good news is that you are perfectly normal. The bad news is you are perfectly normal. *Perfectly normal* equates to being *truly average* and *average* never defines the life of a champion. However, perfectly normal also means that you have the capacity to change! There are ways to overcome fear and live like a champion. As you will see, those ways are paved with purpose.

By definition, courage is the quality of mind or character that enables a person able to face danger, pain, or trouble. It is not that you go though life unconcerned about the dangers that lurk behind the door of opportunity... it's the ability to recognize the danger and risk involved, make the necessary arrangements or adjustments required to give you the best opportunity for success... then with courage, walk through that door.

To better illustrate courage, allow me to introduce you to one of the most influential people I have ever met, my uncle, George W. Alford. Although he is no longer alive, Uncle George was solid in every area of living like a champion including that of exhibiting courage every day. When he was a child, he suffered with osteomyelitis. One of his legs did not grow and develop as the other, leaving him with the need to wear one shoe with a heel built up to allow him to walk somewhat normally.

On another occasion during his youth, while using a knife to cut a piece of string (not knowing how to properly use that knife), he pulled the blade of the knife up toward his face to cut the string. As the knife sliced through the string, the momentum carried it up and into his left eye leaving him blind in that eye for the rest of his life.

With so much working against him, and with reasonable excuses to succumb to fear and give up, he grew into a mighty man of character and became a missionary traveling around the world preaching and ministering to others.

During the summer before my senior year in high school, my family and I went to Denver, Colorado to visit Uncle George. While in Denver, he suggested that we drive to the top of Pike's Peak. Being a native of the flatlands of West Tennessee, upon our ascent to the top, I was amazed at the height and grandeur of Pike's Peak. I was unprepared, however, for what was in store just a few miles up the road. As we got closer to the top, the air became thinner and thinner. At a certain point, the altitude was such that it was impossible for the roads to be paved. We were driving on a gravel road. With the air being so thin, the motor on the Suburban, with the accelerator pressed hard to the floor, could only manage for us to crawl up the mountain at a rate of about 10-15 miles per hour. I was afraid.

My aunt, Uncle George's sister, had made the decision to kneel in the back to pray rather than looking at the edge of the road that seemed to literally drop off into "thin air". The rest of us were watching the road and praying. I guess you could say we were following the direction in Scripture that admonishes us to watch and pray. This went on until someone looked at Uncle George and asked: "Aren't you afraid?"

I will never forget his response. He said: "I may die today, I may not get off this mountain alive but I will never die being afraid; concerned maybe, afraid, never!" Those words still ring out, not only in my ear, but also in my heart today. I may be concerned but I will never be controlled by fear. For the first time I understood what courage was all about. I understood that courage is a choice, a choice that allows me to live as a champion.

"My father's sword upon my side,
He gave it to me the day he died.
I worked for years to become a knight,

83

> ***But not one evildoer did I smite.***
> ***Every time the king sent me out,***
> ***I ran and hid with fear and doubt.***
> ***I wanted to help in the wars,***
> ***But I stayed behind the safety of my doors."***

The knight in our poem is without excuse. He was given the training necessary to become a knight, and his dad gave him his own sword the day he died. He was equipped to live as a champion. The problem was that he allowed fear to override what he already possessed (preparation and weaponry). Swords are made for battle. His dad gave him the sword because he wanted him to fight; to fight for his own honor, the well being of those around him, and for the cause for which he (the father) fought and died. That day he was given a choice: a choice to use his gifts and talents (the sword and the training he had received) for nobility and honor, or to flee from responsibility bestowed upon a knight and forsake the purpose for which his dad lived and died. He had everything necessary to become an honored knight, but the choice he made led him down another road.

How many of us walk along that road like a hapless knight every day we live? Just as the knight, we have what it takes to live as a champion, but we opt for a road that is paved with the promise of safety and security. Many times this road, like the road taken by the knight and the Rams' coach, leads us to the end we dread. The knight died, not in the heat of battle, but on a personal battlefield covered with his fear and inaction. He didn't enter the battlefield himself when he was strong and had the best opportunity to win; he allowed the battle to come to him and he offered no opposition.

What battles are you facing in your life today? Are you using every gift and talent you have to live like a champion every day? What is holding you back? Are you showing up on Game Day or are you trying to avoid risks? Are you a *gamer*, willing to leave it all out on the field? If not, what are the consequences? Historically, the nation of Israel reveals many examples of good and bad choices when it comes to battle. King David fell into the lowest point of his life because he didn't show up for battle. It was the time of year when Kings go to battle and, for whatever reason, David stayed behind in the friendly confines of his castle. He wasn't fulfilling his purpose. One day, while the army of Israel was out on the battlefield, David was walking around on the roof of his castle. David witnessed a sight that led to some fateful decisions. Bathsheba, the beautiful wife of Uriah, was bathing within David's sight and his eyes were full of lust. He requested that she be brought to his chambers where he committed an act with her that he had already committed in his heart... adultery. She became pregnant, and her husband, by order of the king, was ushered to the frontline of the fiercest battle to be killed. What David thought he would never do, he had done. It all started when he ignored his purpose to lead. He chose to stay behind and not show up on the battlefield for Game Day. The game came to him, and, as it turned out, it was not the game he wanted to play.

"The people laughed from time to time,
I felt like I had committed an awful crime.
I watched my father fight and die,
When I ran toward him as I cried.
Ever since then I've been afraid to fight,"

Afraid to fight? How could a young man trained to be a knight be afraid to fight? He tells us in his own words: *"I watched my father fight and die, When I ran to him as I cried."* He witnessed what must have been a horrifying scene... his courageous father fought and died before his very eyes. At that point everything most likely moved in slow motion for him. He was crying and running toward his dad. As he raced to his dad's side, each step he took was filled with both anger and fear; drops of blood spilling from his dad's body matched each teardrop that fell to the ground. Rightly so, at this point in time, he was more concerned about his dad than the battle around him, after all... this was his dad, the knight he had looked up to all of his life, the one who inspired him to be a knight, was dying on the battlefield where he had fought so gallantly. Why my dad? Why here? Why now? So many questions filled his mind... questions seemingly without answers and yet the answer was there all along, only to be found in his dad's purpose. It was purpose that had driven him into battle; a cause so big that he would lay his life down for it. Yet, like many of us, our knight could only see with his eyes, not his heart.

Can we blame him? How many times have we seen others fall in battles, be they physical, mental or spiritual? How has that affected us in our battles? How has it affected our courage? I have witnessed too many people retreating from a battle simply because they have seen someone else fall. What if, as a nation, we *checked out* of the war on terror simply because we have seen so many brave heroes give their lives on that battlefield? What if, as some have suggested, we had not responded to the attack on the World Trade Center and Pentagon on 9/11/01? Where would we be today? What message would we be sending the enemies of freedom?

Just as the young knight needed time to mourn the death of his dad, we, as a nation, needed time to mourn those we lost on that monumental day. But there came a day of decision, the day we either had to make a stand to fight or remain behind, locked in the perceived safety of our castle. The young knight's dad died fighting for a cause, something he believed in. Did that cause end with his death? I think not. His life, his previous battles won, represented his investment in that cause. Did he do this for his son to just give up? No!

The fact that he died in battle tells us that the objective was not yet reached. After a time of mourning, the knight should have taken his dad's sword back into the battle and given his best effort to finish what his dad so valiantly started. What if we had shut down NASA after the death of any one of the heroes who lost their lives on a mission? If we had, we would have never reached the moon. We would not even be thinking of sending an astronaut to the surface of Mars. What if we ignored the terror brought to the forefront of our national consciousness on 9/11/01?

"So soon I will feel the pain of death's bite.
I am now on the battlefield,
But my sword I will not wield.
Even as the arrows fly,
I will not fight even if I die.
My blood now pours out like a river,
Into God's hands my life is delivered."

Our knight finds himself on the battlefield. He will not wield his sword, even as the arrows fly, he will not fight even if he dies. You see, whether we retreat from battle or not, we are still on the battlefield. As long as we are here on earth, there will be daily battles to be fought (and won!). You can check out of the battle, but you can't leave the battlefield. ***You either wield or yield... there are no other options.*** You either wield your sword in battle or yield to the sword of your enemy. Even in the prayers of Jesus as recorded in the Bible, he never prayed that His people be taken out of the battle, but that they would be strengthened in battle. **Every day is Game Day.**

Yes, we will always be on the battlefield, so we must be engaged in the battle. Staying in the battle means much more than physically standing there. It requires the commitment of our bodies, minds and souls.

This point was driven home during a coaching session with a business owner. We were discussing the issue of maintaining purpose. The owner was a former U.S. Navy pilot. He flew several missions taking off from and landing on an aircraft carrier. I asked him a tough question that day about staying on purpose. I said, "If you were on a mission and realized that you either had enough fuel to fly the mission or make it back to the ship what would you do?

Of course I know that naval strategists are precision planners and barring some unforeseen adversity or miscalculation, this would be unlikely; however, I was making a point, so we continued.

He said that he would turn back... I thought, "Me, too!" It was what he said next that intrigued me.

He said, "Of course we would turn back... **if it were a training mission.**" He continued. If we were on a *real* mission, depending on how critical that mission was to our overall national security, we would continue with the mission. That was it! Staying focused on a training mission meant staying alive; while staying focused on a "real life" mission meant meeting the objective. The connection was made! It's all about being focused on purpose!

Courage is connected to purpose. Without it any endeavor can be conquered by fear; with it, fear succumbs to courage. That's why my Uncle George said that he might die concerned but never in fear. It was simply because he lived every minute of his day on purpose.

**Purpose is the Fuel for Courage
...the compass by which we find our direction in life.**

To live every day with courage you must first know your purpose. Much has been written about courage and purpose, but too little has been written about the connection of discovering purpose that results in living every day with courage. The knight in our poem never mentioned purpose. He mentioned the wars and being trained and sent by the king, but never having a purpose. He never mentioned why he became a knight. His dad had courage fueled by purpose, demonstrated when he gave his son his sword. The knight was fearful; he could only see his dad dying on the battlefield. He lacked the courage/purpose connection.

Significant accomplishment always has a price tag. The price of anything purposeless is always too high. *My definition of purpose is that it is the magnetic pull of our internal compass whereby we find our direction in life.* That sense of direction fuels courage. Let's look at two people with courage fueled and directed by purpose: Martin Luther King, and President George W. Bush:

<u>Martin Luther King Jr.</u>

At the age of 35, Martin Luther King, Jr. became the youngest man to ever win the coveted Nobel Peace Prize yet that was not his greatest moment. He is best known for his "I have a dream..." speech delivered on August 28, 1963, before 250,000 people in Washington D.C. on the mall in front of the Lincoln Memorial. It was there that he pushed his carefully prepared speech aside and began to speak from his heart, the heart of a black man who, as a boy, was told by his childhood friend's mother that, because he was black and her child was white, they shouldn't play together. **This was Game Day and the courage of a champion was required.**

"I have a dream deeply rooted in the American Dream. I have a dream that one day this nation will rise up and live out these truths to be self-evident, that all man are created equal.

*I have a dream that my four little children will
one day live in a nation where they will not be judged
by the color of their skin but by the content of their
character. I have a dream..."*

Yet, in all its glory, giving that speech wasn't his greatest
moment. One of his defining moments came when the road-
weary Dr. King told a group of friends, "Sometimes I get
so tired, but I can't stop." Again, this was Game Day, and
the courage of a champion was required. It was purpose that
fueled the courage for him to press on.

Perhaps his greatest moment this side of heaven was
revealed in a statement he made in a sermon he preached
just prior to his death. Only weeks later, a single shot rang
out of the shadows in Memphis, Tennessee that ended the
life of Dr. Martin Luther King, Jr. Although that shot ended
his life, it did not kill his dream. He paid the ultimate price
for his courage; but as we have learned, enduring purpose
comes with a price and he was already paying his dues daily.
Today we celebrate his life because of his courage to stand
for what is right.

On the day of his funeral, thousands of people gathered at
Ebenezer Baptist Church in Atlanta, Georgia to pay tribute to
this great man. During the funeral, many were surprised to hear
his deep voice echo these words spoken just weeks earlier:

*"I'd like someone to mention that day that Martin Luther
King, Jr., tried to give his life serving others. I'd like for
somebody to say that Martin Luther King, Jr., tried to love
somebody."*

Someone had recorded that sermon in those final weeks
of his life. Earlier in the sermon he had mentioned that he
didn't want to be remembered because he'd won a Nobel
Peace Prize, that wasn't important. He had lived his life to the
final day, **on purpose**—a life of courage, a life of direction.

Martin Luther King, Jr. knew that purpose fuels courage and is also the compass by which we find our direction in life. He understood that Game Day is that day in which all of the past culminates with present actions to forever change the future. As a true champion, he knew that every day is Game Day.

President George W. Bush

Moments after the first plane hit the World Trade Center in New York City on the morning of September 11, 2001, word of the tragedy reached President George W. Bush in the hallway of a school in Sarasota, Florida. It was at this school that he was scheduled to meet with second-graders and give a speech on education. Upon hearing the news of the first plane hitting the World Trade center he exited the hallway into a private room where he spoke with National Security Advisor Condoleezza Rice; it appeared at the time that this tragedy could be just a terrible accident. He then proceeded with his itinerary to meet with the second-graders as his team of advisors searched for the truth behind the tragedy.

At precisely 9:04 A.M. EST Chief of Staff Andrew H. Card whispered the chilling news into the Presidents ear that a second plane had hit the other tower of the World Trade Center. At this point it was clear that this was no accident. **This was Game Day and the courage of a champion was required.**

President Bush reached deep inside his heart and soul to deliver this disturbing news to the American people from the very podium in the school's media center where he was scheduled to deliver a speech on education. At 9:30 A.M. he told the American people that there had been "an apparent terrorist attack on our country". Although his plans to deliver a speech in Florida on education that day were changed by this tragedy, hours later, at Barksdale Air Force Base in Louisiana, President Bush did deliver one of the most powerful speeches ever given on education... a lesson in courage.

"Make no mistake: The United States will hunt down and punish those responsible for these cowardly acts... The resolve of our great nation is being tested. But make no mistake: We will show the world that we will pass this test. God Bless."

That was not the only education in courage speech he gave that day. Although urged not to go back to Washington and the White House, President Bush said that the nation needed to see their President in the White House in our nation's capital.

Later that night, back in Washington, in the Oval Office of the White House, President Bush addressed the nation again:

"...Today, our fellow citizens, our way of life, our very freedom came under attack in a series of deliberate and deadly terrorist acts. The victims were in airplanes or in their offices: secretaries, business men and women, military and federal workers, moms and dads, friends and neighbors.

Thousands of lives were suddenly ended by evil, despicable acts of terror. The pictures of airplanes flying into buildings, fires burning, huge structures collapsing have filled us with disbelief, terrible sadness and a quiet, unyielding anger.

These acts of mass murder were intended to frighten our nation into chaos and retreat. But they have failed. Our country is strong. A great people have been moved to defend a great nation.

Terrorist attacks can shake the foundations of our biggest buildings, but they cannot touch the foundation of America. These acts shatter steel, but they cannot dent the steel of American resolve.

America was targeted for attack because we're the brightest beacon for freedom and opportunity in the world. And no one will keep that light from shining.

Today, our nation saw evil, the very worst of human nature, and we responded with the best of America, with the daring of our rescue workers, with the caring for strangers and neighbors who came to give blood and help in any way they could.

...The search is underway for those who are behind these evil acts.

I've directed the full resources for our intelligence and law enforcement communities to find those responsible and bring them to justice. We will make no distinction between the terrorists who committed these acts and those who harbor them.

...America and our friends and allies join with all those who want peace and security in the world and we stand together to win the war against terrorism. Tonight I ask for your prayers for all those who grieve, for the children whose worlds have been shattered, for all whose sense of safety and security has been threatened. And I pray they will be comforted by a power greater than any of us spoken through the ages in Psalm 23: "Even though I walk through the valley of the shadow of death, I fear no evil for you are with me."

This is a day when all Americans from every walk of life unite in our resolve for justice and peace. America has stood down enemies before, and we will do so this time. None of us will ever forget this day, yet we go forward to defend freedom and all that is good and just in our world.

Thank you. Good night and God bless America.

On that day, we as a nation were brought together, united in a way we had not been since the attack on Pearl Harbor. Champions know that purpose is fuel for courage and the compass by which we find our direction in life. They have the courage to stay the course and follow that direction. They understand that Game Day is that day in which all of the past culminates with present actions to forever change the future. They know that Every Day is Game Day.

The Common Thread

Martin Luther King, Jr. and President George W. Bush and my Uncle George all had one thing in common... PURPOSE. That was the fuel for courage and the compass by which they found direction in life. Through purpose, they understood that Game Day is that day in which the past culminates with present actions to forever change the future. They understood that Every Day is Game Day!

Now what about you? Where is your courage? What did you discover about purpose and courage in chapters three and four? What is your fuel for courage to do what you are driven to do? What is your compass by which you find direction in life? Do you understand that Game Day is that day in which all of the past culminates with present actions to forever change the future? Do you realize that today is Game Day? What you did or didn't do yesterday affects you today. What you do or don't do today will shape your tomorrow. Decide to take action today that will put you in a position to live better tomorrow.

In the next chapter you will gain an in-depth understanding of how to marry purpose and courage, by discovering a clear and concise vision that will guide your journey to fulfillment. You will find an action plan to help you clearly articulate that vision to others so they will not only catch your vision, but be fellow-travelers on the road to success!

So, if you are ready to take one more step in the direction of living like a winner every day, complete the Power Plays at the end of this chapter and then **read on, champion!**

Power Plays – Chapter 4

-Make a list of your fears. Which fears do you have that prompt you into action? – In-action?

-What opportunities have you missed in life because of fear?

-Describe how your life would be different if you could overcome or more effectively deal with fear.

-From the list of fears above, which fear(s) prevent you from living out your purpose?

-Review your purpose statement from Chapter 3.

-Document which fear(s), listed above outweigh your purpose. Which fear(s) listed above do you consider to be more important to you than your purpose?

-Note: If there is even one fear listed in response to the question above, go back to chapter 3 (re-read if neces- sary) to discover your true purpose. No fear should outweigh your true purpose. Notice I said "outweigh"… the fear may still be present, but it takes a backseat to your ability to live on purpose.

CHAPTER 5

Champions Practice the Principles of 4-Dimensional Vision

———❦———

Champions understand the distinction between wishing and hoping. You may have never thought about it that way, but there is a significant difference. My parents have a tape recording of me as a child saying, "I wish I had a million dollars." Was that a *goal* I was striving for at the time? No, I was only *wishing* I had a million dollars. A goal is an expected result or achievement within a certain time frame toward which effort is directed. I wanted it then and I didn't want to have to do anything to get it. Neither did I set a date by which I wanted to have the money. I just wanted it to appear. So, was there a chance that a million dollars was about to appear in my bank account at that time? I didn't say that I hope to have a million dollars. Should I have had even a glimmer of hope? Of course I didn't have any hope or expectation that I would suddenly have a million dollars in the bank. I didn't even have a bank account to put it in. So, why would there be any hope for that to happen? I had done nothing other than wish for it.

By definition, a wish means that we have a desire for something. Did I have a desire for a million dollars? Well, that's what I said I wanted when I made the wish. Yet, I didn't have a basis for the hope that I would have a million dollars. There is an added element when we consider the definition of the word *hope*. In the intransitive sense, *hope* means to cherish a desire with anticipation. In the transitive sense, hope is defined as having a desire with expectation of obtainment, or, to expect with confidence. Did you catch the difference? To *wish* is to have a desire for; whereas to hope is to cherish a desire with anticipation... to desire with expectation of obtainment... to expect with confidence.

In the case of hope, there is an implied element of action that allows me to desire with anticipation; to have an expectation of obtainment with confidence. In other words, hope implies that there is a reason for my expectation... a wish joined with a reason to believe.

So what is it that gives me a reason to believe? Great question; I'm glad you asked! It's all about cause and effect. Sometimes during lunch, while working out at the gym, I see people coming through for a tour with one of the certified fitness trainers. They are walking around looking at the equipment, asking the trainer questions about gym membership. Most share one thing in common—that look in their eyes. They all seem to have that far away stare, and I'm confident that they are thinking the same thing I thought when I took my first tour of the gym. As is the case with most people, they are probably thinking: "This is where I am going to totally transform my body. It's going to be different. This time I'm really going to do it right."

Some never join, while others join only to go for a few workouts and quit working out when they become tired or bored with the slow process of getting in shape. The problem is that, after they join or come a few times, I don't see most of them around the gym three months later. There are some, however, who join, stick with it and start to see changes within several weeks or a few months.

What's the difference in these people? I truly believe that some stopped at just *wishing* while others took consistent action that gave them reason to have *hope*. The difference between wishing and hoping is the act of doing something to substantiate and sustain that reason for hope. Although taking that first action like joining the gym is important, I believe there is a little-known factor that really makes a long-term difference (not just in people working out in gyms) for everyone who truly makes that transformation from wishing to hoping. That little-known factor is *Visualization*. This is a fundamental step that gives people reason to transcend wishing to obtain legitimate hope.

In Solomon's writing of Proverbs (29:18 KJV), he says, "Where there is no vision, the people perish." The New International Version states: "the people cast off restraint". Where there is no vision, there is no hope, where there is no hope, people perish. It could very well be that they perish because they cast off restraint. Casting off restraint makes me think about people with a lack of self-discipline. The reverse also seems to be true. Where there is vision, people thrive. They use restraint or self-discipline as an ally. They are focused on realizing the vision.

One of the most important processes that we use at Building Champions early in the coaching process is the creation of a clear *vision*. In fact, vision is one element of what we call *The Core Four*, which includes: the Life Plan; Vision; Business Plan, and Priority Management. All four are used throughout the coaching process. The vision is the second piece of the Core Four, right after the Life Plan. This vision is the greatest tool I have as a coach that inspires my clients to higher levels of excellence and accountability.

After all, it is the vision that clearly defines where they want to take their business.

Vision is not only for business owners. It can be used with any individual. If you work you need to have a vision for your work. In the span of my career, I can think of at least five positions where the vision I had allowed me to develop that position into more than the job I was hired to do. Of course, the rewards and accolades followed. Still, it was my vision, and that vision kept me working in the direction of taking the position beyond the original job description given to me when I was hired. Many times that allowed me to help other people do the same in their positions. Needless to say, each time, my employer was well pleased.

I like to call visualizing *"Time Machine Thinking"* because during the process of discovering and documenting your vision, you are not only allowed, but encouraged to put yourself in a mental time machine and to move forward to a new time and place where you have accomplished all your desires in terms of your career. You can, and should, make believe that you are already there. We will discuss this more in the components of vision, but for now, just know that you are about to take the journey of your life (at least in your mind). You too, can develop your career into more than you've ever dreamed possible; it can be done starting with the power of vision.

How to Get Started

Getting started with vision is simple, but it takes time. First you should find a place conducive to creative thinking, a place you would like to invest four to six hours in the discovery and creation of your vision. You should find a location that is convenient, yet away from distractions. Many people find that they get their best work done at *Starbucks* or a local bookstore. Others may feel the need to find a quieter place such as a school library, or maybe even a cabin in the mountains. The point is that you need to be where you can focus on what you want in terms of your business or career. Once you find the best place to develop your vision, you will need to schedule an appointment with yourself and make others aware of the importance of this appointment. You should let nothing short of a family emergency deter you from keeping this appointment. Just realize that this one appointment could mean the difference between unbelievable success in your work life and a life of mediocrity.

There is not a lot of pre-work that needs to be done before you arrive. Most of the work has already been done in your heart. That's right, the real secret is that you are not about to *develop* your vision; you are about to *discover* it. Your vision is already written in the recesses of your heart. You are just working to unveil it and get it on paper. Again, you are not developing a vision; you are discovering the vision and developing a document around that discovery.

Components of Vision

To review, there is a difference between wishing and hoping. A powerfully documented vision is much more than a statement of what you wish will happen. It carries much more weight. A powerfully written vision is simply the outcome of a discovery process that reaches deep into your heart.
In an impressively written article for the *Harvard Business Review*, Jim Collins addressed four components of a well-constructed vision. They are:

1) Core Values;
2) Core Purpose;
3) B.H.A.G. (Big Hairy Audacious Goals) at Building Champions, we call these *Mount Everest Goals*, and
4) Vivid Description.

Let's consider each carefully.

Core Values

Each of us has a set of *core values*, or strongly held beliefs. They are actually the guardians of our conscience. We would not violate these strongly held beliefs or values even if it meant losing a deal, losing money, or the threat of losing your job. These beliefs that you will never sacrifice or violate comprise your core values or core convictions.

One of the first things you will need to do while working on your vision is to take a *heart inventory* to examine what you believe to be most important and list them as your core values. There are many ways to do this; one example can be found on our web site at www.gamedaychampions.com.

Core Purpose

Core Purpose is a statement that represents the essence of why you do what you do and the reasons for your actions. This is what gives meaning to your work. It's your reason for being as it relates to your career. You may recall, as you read in Chapter 3: Champions Live Every Day with Purpose, we considered the fact that purpose begins to come into focus at the point where desire intersects with potential. The same is true for your statement of core purpose in vision.

In terms of your career, you do what you do today because of some combination of desire and potential. You are able to do what you do because someone saw potential in you during the interview or selection process. You choose to do what you do today because of some desire. Think about it like this: although you may or may not want to do what you are doing right now in terms of your career, you are there because of an original desire to be there. That desire may be driven by the fact that this is the only job you have available right now and you need the money. Hopefully it is not that extreme. However, the exciting aspect of vision is that it is a dynamic, changing process that can actually light your fire. Vision is the key to realizing that tomorrow doesn't have to look like today. To a great extent you have the ability to script your tomorrows.

Mount Everest Goals
Big Hairy Audacious Goals

There aren't many people in the world who have climbed Mount Everest. After watching *Vertical Limit* (a stunning movie about mountain climbing), and thinking about *Into Thin Air* (an incredible book about people lost while climbing) as well as other similar books and movies, I have decided that climbing Mount Everest is not one of my goals. I climbed a little hill in Colorado that seemed like a mountain to me. We weren't really all that high, but to my humidity-conditioned southern lungs, I felt like I was high enough. I could barely breathe. I wanted to quit several times but didn't.

As we reached the top my friend, Todd Duncan, who was climbing with us, knew I was writing this book. He suggested that we take a picture of me at the summit (with even higher possible summits in the background). He said that it would make a great picture for the book jacket. Needless to say, because of the way I looked after the climb, that picture neither made the jacket of this book nor will it be on the jacket of any other book. The idea Todd had was great... it could have been perfect, but I had given almost everything I had inside of me to get to the top of that little hill, and that exhaustion shows in the picture. Although I do not plan to actually climb Mount Everest, I do have Mount Everest-type goals. These are goals that are bigger than life; goals that are actually so huge they almost create their own gravity.

These are goals that drive me upward. Jim Collins calls them BHAG's (Big Hairy Audacious Goals); at Building Champions, we call them Mount Everest Goals. I'm sure you have your own Mount Everest Goals, and those goals should be clearly documented in your vision.

Vivid Description

After the Mount Everest Goals are clear and documented in the vision, the final step is to have some fun painting the future. A *Vivid Description* is simply a portrait of what the future will look like after you achieve your goals. It's painted in as much detail as possible with words by you, and reflects exactly how you want the future to look. When the vivid description is completed, it's a good idea to make a list of the statements you have made describing the future that are different from present reality. This list of statements becomes the blueprint from which you work to make the transformation from current reality to fruition of the vision. This is your gap list. This blueprint, or gap list, will help you isolate those areas that need attention. This includes projects you need to do and a list of your plan for strictly- adhered-to daily, weekly and monthly disciplines. When all steps are constructed and completed you have fruition. This fruition of a vision then fosters an even greater, far-reaching vision. At this point you are hopping from peak to peak and summit to summit.

Vision in 4 Dimensions

In order to assist with vision discovery and development, I developed a process I call the *4-Dimensional Vision Process*. This process consists of 4 D's:

1) Discovery;
2) Development;
3) Display, and
4) Deployment.

Discovery

At some point over the past few years, I realized that great visions aren't developed, they are discovered. This is true for individuals as well as teams. I realized that, for the most part, individuals and leaders of groups say they want others to "buy in" to their vision. After hearing this over and over, it dawned on me that, in many cases, that's what they get, however it isn't necessarily what they want. My contention is that "buy in" only gets you what I like to call "passive support". People will "buy in" to your vision, or go along with it for two basic reasons: 1) they like you as a person or a leader, or 2) they are afraid of you. The fact is that they just "buy in" to and passively go along with the vision. The passive support you get isn't going to get you to the summit of any Mount Everest Goal.

After realizing that "buy in" is never enough, it occurred to me that's what individuals and leaders really need is for others to be "*souled* out" to their vision. When people are *souled* out to the vision, the new dynamic experienced is heartfelt. *Passionate Pursuit* of a vision comes from people who are "souled out" and has a radically positive effect. When people passively support a vision, little gets done; progress is usually made, but it is only a shadow of what can be. When people passionately pursue the vision, heaven and earth seem to move in their favor at times.

This is where it really gets fun. In order to explore this topic further, we will need to consider it from two different viewpoints: 1) that of an individual, and 2) that of a leader.

Discovery for Individuals

For the most part, it's hard enough to get other people to adequately "buy in" to your vision much less "sell out" to it. However, for the individual, this is more of an inside job. You have to personally be "sold out" to your vision long before you should expect anyone else to be at that level of passion. Too many people merely "buy in" to and passively support their own visions. Only champions totally "sell out" to their own visions. What a sad statement to make... few people passionately pursue their own vision! If you don't believe this, all it takes is a quick look around. How many true champions do you know? Compare that to how many people are sitting around wishing something good would happen to them?

You have to be passionate about your own vision, and if you aren't then you haven't fully discovered what that vision is, and you must dig deeper. You must keep on digging until you find whatever invokes a burning passion that will cause you to completely sell out. Selling out to your vision isn't about totally dying to the rest of the world. Your first priority is to your Life Plan and all of those critical accounts you have listed. However, selling out to your vision has everything to do with saying "no" to those distracting temptations that try to pull you away from your best self. That happens to all of us, champions included. The only difference is that when it comes to their Life Plan and their Business or Career Vision, champions let nothing short of personal illness or family emergencies pull them off task.

At this point I must stop to be sure you totally understand what I am saying, as well as what I'm not saying. I am saying that to accomplish your vision, you must be fueled by passion. If you are not passionate about your vision, you have not truly discovered your vision. I am not saying that you should allow your vision for your career override your life and those areas, or accounts that should be given more attention than your business or career. Too many times people have sold out to their careers only to realize in the end that they got what they wanted at work, but lost what they really needed at home. This too is about lasting priorities.

When I said that champions don't let anything get in the way of their vision, I did not say that they overrode their values to find fruition in their vision. Remember there are 4 steps to vision and Core Values always come before Mount Everest Goals.

Discovery for Leaders

When it comes to leading people, the Discovery piece of the 4-Dimensional Vision Process can be one of the most powerful investments you can make in your career, and the people you lead. The opportunity is endless and the possibilities are almost unimaginable. I know that is a huge statement to make, but it is true. The sky truly is the limit.

People want to follow a leader with a vision, and people want to be part of that vision. As human beings, we are wired to want to be part of something special. We want to feel as though we are contributing in a positive way to something bigger than ourselves. This is one principle that too many leaders never grasp. However, it is one of the simplest things a leader can do, and it only takes a little intestinal fortitude.

After the original vision has been documented, the next thing a leader should do is to have a "Vision Discovery" meeting with his / her team. With a current copy of the existing vision in hand, the leader should share that vision with the team and then follow with a statement that will not only catch most people by surprise, but open the door to endless rows of low hanging fruit. The statement goes something like this: "As the _____ (fill in the blank with whatever position the leader holds), this is the vision that I have for where I believe we can and should go; however, I realize that two (or more) heads are better than one, and that you, as members of this team, can help me make it even better. I have a few questions I want to ask that I hope will promote further discussion and will allow us to develop a much more powerful vision."

At this point, the leader will proceed with questions such as these:

- How good can we really be?
- How much can we really accomplish together?
- How can we make what we do more fun?
- How can we make it easier on each other, as well as on those we serve?
- How much of a "Wow" impact can we have on the people we serve, as well as each other?
- How can we show other people how good we really are?

Those questions, as well as other starter questions you will find at www.gamedaychampions.com , really open the hearts and minds of team members. The very act of asking the questions allows the team to see the heart of the leader, and allows the leader to see the heart of the team. I have followed this approach myself several times with some astounding results. However, without fail, every time I ask a coaching client to have a "Discovery" meeting like this, I detect an element of fear. I even experienced some level of fear myself the first time I did it. However, the results of fostering and tapping collegiality are immense, and it is difficult to describe the euphoria that you feel as a leader when it is a challenge to find a stopping-point for the "Discovery" meeting. It's always a joy for me to hear my Building Champions clients report back with excitement telling me how the meeting went... and that's just step one of the 4D Vision Process!

Development

It's in the development stage that most people really start the vision process. This stage is really the second phase of the process. As you know, the only place to start is in discovery. However, the development piece of the puzzle is extremely important. It's here that all of the scattered thoughts from the Discovery stage are pulled together and synthesized into a logical written document. You can think about it like an accordion, the discovery stage is wide open... the more ideas the better; whereas the development stage pulls it all back together into one nice and neat document.

In some cases with the discovery stage, quantity is more important than quality. In fact, that is one of the standard rules of brainstorming... more is better. That's okay because one wild and crazy thought can lead to deeper thinking in some areas resulting in a better overall outcome. One idea can lead to another. People can actually "hitch-hike" from a wild and crazy idea to one that is highly effective and easily implemented.

However, it's in the development stage that a clear and concise written vision is developed. The desired outcome of this stage is that written vision that encapsulates all that was addressed in discovery in such a way that everyone on the team knows that they were instrumental in the formation of the final written vision. This is not to say that every idea is mentioned or addressed in the vision, it's just that everyone knows they played an integral role, or at least were given the opportunity to play an integral role in the formation of the vision. If this is the case, you have just moved one step closer to people being sold out to the vision.

For individual visions, the individual knows that he/ she has thoroughly rehearsed the options and angles to give himself / herself the best opportunity to proceed and succeed.

Display

At this point, proceeding simply means that you are ready to consider how the journey *from here to there* will be depicted. In other words, this is the stage where you determine how you will clearly show where you started, and where you are in relation to where you want to be. Think of this mapping process as the *scoreboard stage*. This is where those key numbers will be tallied.

If you have ever been to a sporting event, you know there is a scoreboard that indicates the vital statistics of the game you were watching. Let's take football for example. During the course of the game there are numbers that tell the story of the game. For example, a scoreboard in football not only records the score of the game, but in addition, the time left in the game, the number of time outs remaining for each team, the yard line upon which the ball rests, the down count, the number of yards to a first down, and so on. You get the picture literally by looking at the scoreboard.

In this stage it is important that all involved know what is being measured, why it is being measured, and what will be done as a result of certain measurements. It's long been said, "that which gets measured, gets improved". The same is true about the display stage of the 4 D Vision Process. At this point, everyone involved has played a role in defining the desired end-results, so it's only natural that the journey from start to finish is recorded, and observed by all interested parties.

Back in the days of W. Edwards Deming and Joseph Juran, the Japanese used these principles of tracking results to totally transform the manufacturing world. What once was looked upon as "cheap junk" quickly became the Lexus', Toyotas, Nissans, Hondas and Mazdas of today. Soon people were willing to pay a premium for that "Made in Japan" label. By tracking key results, learning from the process and making the necessary adjustments, they were able to manufacture premium products, and you can too. You can design, develop and create greater efficiencies and quality in your life as you use the display stage to your benefit by analyzing the results and making the necessary adjustments.

Deployment

The deployment stage is the fourth and final stage in the 4 - D Vision Process. You may have heard the statement "last but not least"; that certainly applies to the deployment stage. Up until this stage, everything else in the 4 – D Vision Process has been talk and set-up. Although you certainly can't get the results you want without the first three steps, you won't get anything without deployment. This is where the rubber hits the road; it's the execution or implementation stage.

It's in this stage that you will implement the disciplines that you have recognized to be so vital to your success. It's here that you will actually work on projects and get things done. In the end, the results of what is done in deployment will clearly be depicted in the display stage, and that should reflect what was agreed to in discovery and documented in the development stage. It all comes together here.

The Parallel Universe to the 4 – D Vision Process

Sadly, there is a parallel universe to the 4 – D Vision Process. The 4 D's associated with this parallel universe are:

1) Denial
2) Despondency
3) Discouragement
4) Despair

Obviously this is not where you want to be. Although, if you really think about it, the natural progression depicted in this parallel universe begins with denial, which leads to despondency, after that comes discouragement (the courage is actually sucked out of you), and then finally complete and utter despair. The only way around finding yourself in this "Twilight Zone" type vortex is to follow the true 4-Dimensional Approach to Vision. In addition to the Power Play at the end of this chapter, you can find more information and tools concerning the 4 –Dimensional Approach to Vision at www.gamedaychampions.com .

In the next chapter we will discuss the importance of planning... Champions Plan to Win. What's your plan?

Power Plays – Chapter 5

- Now that I shared with you one of my childhood wishes, what is your secret wish or wishes? Write your list of wishes in your Champion's Journal.

- Describe your reason for hope. What have you done that gives you hope that your wish or wishes will come true?

- Review your original action lists from Chapters 1-3. What have you not done that you need to do? When will that action or those actions be completed? Why are you waiting? (Procrastination is the space in time between inspiration and implementation.)

- Note: Chapters 5 and 6 work in conjunction to lay the framework for completing your Life Plan, Business Vision and Business Plan. The Power Plays at the end of Chapter 6 will guide you through the process.

Champions Plan to Win!

———∞∞∞———

The Importance of Planning

Champions plan to win. Have you ever watched a championship game in any sporting event where only moments after the end of the game, the players on the winning team are sporting hats and tee shirts proclaiming their team as champions? Have you ever wondered how they do that so quickly? Those shirts and hats are already printed and sitting in boxes just waiting for the end of the game and for the champions to pull them out of the box and put them on. Funny thing... I've never seen second-place hats or tee shirts. There is a good reason: they are never printed. Shirts and hats are pre-printed for each team as champions... the boxes containing the winner's shirts and hats are opened; the loser's boxes are destroyed. Every team should enter a championship game believing that they will emerge as champions when the game is over. Champions plan—but they don't plan on losing. They plan on winning! Sometimes winning and losing is ordained in the fabric of the plan.

Preparing to win is a pivotal stage in the game of living like a champion every day. First there is the pure mental process of discovering the vision, and at some point there is the execution stage where things get done and results are realized. But sandwiched between those two, in that transitional time, is where the game of championship living is either won or lost. It's called the plan.

If *Every Day is Game Day*, one might ask, when is there time to plan? That's a great question. Champions are always planning their next move. Think about any sporting event you have witnessed. Preparation, or planning, never ends. There is pre-game planning as well as in-game strategy, half time adjustments... and even a 2-minute drill pre-planned for football.

Champions treat planning time just as anyone else would treat game time. "They plan their work and work their plan." They do it prior to the actions they take, as well as during the process of their day. It's like playing chess; the veteran chess master can draw on the experience of previous matches to strategize and make the right moves. Golfer Arnold Palmer once said, "It's a funny thing; the more I practice, the luckier I get."

When traveling on an airplane, it is comforting to know that prior to take-off, a flight plan has been filed. Additionally, throughout the flight there are in-flight checks and corrections to ensure that the flight is proceeding according to that plan. It's like mini-plans within the big plan.

For example, during the process of writing this book, although I started with an outline or plan, I had to make adjustments along the way; adjustments that called for a plan within a plan. While writing each chapter, I thought of specific examples that I wanted to include. Research had to be done, as well as planning, to determine how and where I would use those examples within a chapter.

Planning is integral to each facet of championship living. Champions begin with a broad plan to achieve positive results. A plan is simply the road map that directs us to our destination (goal). Throughout the process, activities are executed or modified to allow for new input. This dynamic approach is a "work in progress," or, as Madison Avenue admen would say, a product that is *new* and *improved*. In the end, champions are life-, career-, and daily-planners.

You may have heard the saying: "If you fail to plan, you are planning to fail." That's why an entire chapter on planning is included in a book that is focused on living every day like a champion. Too many people consider planning to be a passive activity. Planning, when done correctly, is one of the most aggressive and demanding activities required in living life like a champion. There are varied reasons why people don't plan, but the fact remains, for the most part, people don't plan. The lack of planning explains why most people do not live at a championship level.

Champions realize, as my friend and best-selling author, Todd Duncan, states: "If there is anything happening in their lives or businesses that they don't want to happen, or if anything is not happening in their lives and businesses that they want to happen, it's their fault." They take total responsibility. Yes, I realize that there will be unforeseen circumstances that are completely out of our control. Yet, the act of taking full responsibility lends itself to a personal inventory that allows for growth and eliminates the blame game or acceptance of the status quo.

I remember several examples of this from my softball-playing days. Our team was really good (although, admittedly, sometimes my memory *over-serves* me). Over a two-year period we only lost two games in league play. We looked forward to games to the extent that we were truly upset when a game was rained out. We wanted to play. Although this usually wasn't the case for our opponent, we didn't want to reschedule any games. On several occasions, on the afternoon of a game that was about to be cancelled because of a wet field, we gathered together with rakes and shovels in hand. We dug trenches to drain the water off the infield, and then we brought in dry dirt and sand to fill the holes. We raked the new playing surface so that it would be just as though there had been no rain. Afterwards, we would get approval from the league to play the game as scheduled. In many cases, the opposing teams were surprised that the game was not cancelled. You see, we couldn't do anything about the weather... we couldn't prevent the rain... but we could develop a plan and carry out the necessary actions to side step the effects of what we couldn't control. I don't remember ever losing one of those games.

In this chapter we will look at three indispensable tools to make planning an integral part of every day. You will learn how to take advantage of your plans to the extent that you can overcome some once-believed un-preventable snags. The three concrete tools are:

> 1) The Life Plan
> 2) The Business or Career Plan
> 3) The Daily Plan

The Life Plan

One of the most important things we do at Building Champions is also one of the first things we do. We help our clients establish a *Life Plan*. Sadly, most people invest more time in planning for a holiday meal or one-week vacation than they do planning their lives. As coaches, we know that although the primary reason people hire a business coach is to help them increase their business effectiveness, there are elements outside of that business which have a huge impact on what they are able to do in the workplace.

Those elements, or accounts, are the areas of life that are most important to them. For example, if a client is having relationship difficulties outside of business, these issues influence the work environment negatively by reducing effectiveness and productivity.

Daniel Harkavy, our CEO and Head Coach at Building Champions puts it like this: Success in life and business is determined by one critical skill set – decision-making. This is the ability to determine when, where, why and how to do things. If you make the right decisions (or have the right plan) you aren't reacting to what life throws at you. When things aren't going well on the life side, you will bring a less passionate and less focused you to work. In contrast, your own game will improve by having a good plan, which is supported by good and healthy pressure on yourself to do better.

If a client has an unhealthy lifestyle, these habits result in lost days of energy and a lack of focus. The effect home-life has on business is powerful and the reverse is also true. Good disciplines based on a good plan can lead to the fulfill-ment of your goals.

One Totally Awesome Coach

To illustrate, Michelle was a coach at Building Champions who exemplified the effectiveness of a well-written and closely followed Life Plan. Before she became a coach, Michelle was a client of another coach. As it is with all coaching clients, Michelle was led through the process of developing her own Life Plan. During the process of devel-oping her Life Plan, Michelle wrote about how she wanted to be remembered after her life on this earth ended. In her Life Plan she wrote about the ones she wanted to be remem-bered by, and the things that she wanted those people to remember about her. Within the life planning process, she also listed certain things that she wanted to accomplish in each area of her life and the actions necessary to accomplish those things.

Although Michelle was writing about what she wanted to transpire after her life on this earth had ended, the plan included what she would be doing on a daily, weekly and monthly basis that would empower her to live the life she wanted to live. She did just that. Michelle lived her life according to the plan she had developed, and saw the results she wanted to see. Her life, however, wasn't nearly as long as Michelle expected, nor as long as the rest of us wanted. While touring Tuscany on vacation with her husband Chuck and several friends, Michelle had an accident on a *Vespa* motor scooter that abruptly ended her 44 years on this earth. After being airlifted to a hospital where she was in surgery for hours, Michelle's life was soon over, but not her influence.

As Michelle was living her life according to the plan she developed, she impacted so many people in such a positive way, and her influence continues. It was obvious at her memorial service that she was remembered by the people she wanted to be remembered by in ways that she wanted to be remembered. By living her life according to the plan she developed, Michelle had a huge positive impact on lives that are still being influenced today. You can do the same!

In the *Power Play* at the end of this chapter, you will be given the opportunity to develop your own Life Plan. The Life Plan tool you will find consists of a series of questions that will allow you to discover the *accounts* most important in your life. *Accounts* are just those 7-10 areas of life that matter most to you. I say discover because that is exactly what you do. There are pre-established areas that matter most to you... some are evident (they have already been discovered), while some may be dormant (waiting to be discovered). One of my favorite author / speakers is Jim Rohn. He states that there are roughly a half dozen areas that represent the majority of your success in life and business... at Building Champions, we call these the Life Plan Accounts.

Life Plan accounts represent the cornerstone of the plan. Everything centers on these accounts. There are a few Life Plan accounts that I call core, and they appear in almost every Life Plan. They include: Family, Health, Financial, Spiritual, and Career. Although many accounts are the same as those found in other people's Life Plans, some are as different as the people who list them.

I had one client in California who had "Falconry" as a Life Plan account. He told me that he had two falcons and he loved to take them to tournaments. He said that those falcons were very important to him. Your Life Plan is about you and what is important to you. The purpose is to allow yourself to develop a plan that will support you as you strive to reach various goals in the key areas established by you.

In using the tool, you will develop a purpose statement for each account. You will clearly state why that account plays such an important role in your life. You will then document your goal for each specific account. In other words, you will write a time-line, stating where you expect to be in regard to each account at some point in the future.

The final piece that is included in the Life Plan is a list of activities (disciplines) that you know you need to cultivate in order to "arrive on time" at each station.

The outline for life planning is as follows:

Life Plan Outline

- Determine a day and time that you can commit at least six to eight hours to the development of your Life Plan and schedule that time as if it were the most important meeting for you this year.
- Determine a location that would be conducive to creative thinking (as with the vision, this could be at Starbucks, a local bookstore, a hotel or lodge with a great view, or anywhere that holds a special place in your heart).

- Take with you the tool found at my Website, www.game-daychampions.com, inspirational music, your journal(s), any books that may inspire you, as well as any pictures you may have that would stimulate your thinking about how you want life to be.
- After answering the questions, list the seven to ten areas that are most important to you in your life (these are your Life Plan Accounts).
- For each account, determine and clearly define where you want to be in regards to that specific account in 5-10-15 years.
- Determine and clearly define in one or two sentences your purpose for each account listed. Why is that account important to you and what is your specific role for that account?
- List 3-5 disciplines or specific actions that you know you need to commit to, that if done, would help you to live on purpose and achieve your goals within that particular account.
- When the Life Plan is completed, commit to reading it every day for 90 days and then at least weekly thereafter.

When properly developed and followed, the Life Plan can be one of the most positive influences you have ever had in your life, and the time invested to create it can be remembered as one of the most productive times in your life. This is your life, and the Life Plan that you create is the blueprint for how you want to live it. Write it, own it, and live it!

The Business – or – Career Plan

Once the Life Plan and Business Vision (see Chapter 5 for Vision) are completed you are ready to develop the business or career plan. Although there is probably an account in

124

your Life Plan that covers career, you will need to go a little deeper on the business side and the Business Plan tool will help you do just that. At Building Champions, we have found that there are three basic elements in the business planning process, they are:

1) Know your numbers
2) Disciplines
3) Projects

Know Your Numbers

If you've ever been to an emergency room you have probably noticed that soon after the admitting clerk takes the insurance information, the attending care providers will proceed to take certain physical measurements known as vital signs. Included in these vital signs are blood pressure, heart rate and body temperature. The point is that, regardless of the nature of the medical emergency, certain vital signs (or numbers) tell a story that the care providers need to know in order to proceed with the appropriate treatment. The same is true with any business endeavor. There are vital signs or significant numbers associated with every business that, when known, can provide for a quick assessment of the health of a company.

Although there should be no doubt concerning the importance of knowing these numbers when it comes to business planning, many people skip this part. Throughout my years of coaching I have been amazed at the number of people, especially sales people, who do not know the vital numbers associated with their success or failure. Champions, however, know their numbers and are prepared to make adjustments based on need and opportunity. Too many people are just flying by the seat of their pants, which is hardly a way to be successful. People who somehow *fall into* success would be so much more successful if they would determine to know what their numbers are and what they mean.

Disciplines

Although we discuss the importance of disciplines elsewhere in this book, the process of being self-disciplined is so important that it needs to be addressed in this chapter. In the business planning model you are presented in the Power Play available at the end of this chapter, you are asked to list the daily, weekly, and monthly disciplines that you believe will benefit you in your quest to reach your goals. Along with listing those disciplines, you are asked to name a person who will hold you accountable to that discipline.

Accountability means different things to different people, and people respond differently to various levels of accountability. Some people respond better to a whack on the side of the head, whereas others respond better to a gentle nudge. Only you know which level of accountability you would respond to best. It's your responsibility to find someone who will hold you accountable in a way that is most productive for you. Many find the appropriate level of accountability in coaching. The key is to establish accountability with someone other than yourself.

I have had coaching clients who wanted to be solely responsible for their accountability rather than enlisting the help of a friend or relative (or coach for that matter). In each case, I let them know that if they try to be self-accountable, then they are the only one they will need to get approval from for neglecting a specific task or discipline, and that's the only person they are responsible to report to if they ignore a discipline. The bottom line is that without an accountability partner there is no real accountability and a person's disciplines are vulnerable to severe compromise and eventual failure.

Projects

Projects are another area addressed in the Business Plan. Disciplines are on going; they are consistently repeated on a daily, weekly or monthly basis. Projects are, for the most part, one-time endeavors. Projects are started and completed then new projects are started and completed. Projects address areas that need to be established, eliminated, improved or reduced. A target is set, plans are established and acted upon, measurements are taken throughout the process and results are recorded. When the target is reached, the project is finished. In the business plan, you will see a section set aside to list the projects that you need to undertake.

The key to great project work is great planning. One huge step is to have everything you need close to you when you begin to work on a project. Tim Broadhurst, a mortgage planner in Austin, Texas, developed one of the best systems I have encountered concerning equipping himself. Tim developed a three-ring binder in which he keeps all of his project work in tabs. He sets up a tab in the binder for each open project he is working on at the time. As you can imagine, this binder is fairly large so he can't reasonably carry it with him at all times. So he has developed a discipline to carry with him a letter size legal pad with three holes pre-punched so that he can easily transfer his thoughts, etc. from the pad to his binder. He will write on one sheet information and ideas that are associated with a specific project. If he has an idea that pertains to a different project, he will record that information on a different page. When he returns to his office, he simply tears the sheets out of the pad and places them in the appropriate tab in his binder. He invests the first Friday of each month to work on projects. When it's time to work on projects, he will only need to take his binder with him and he will have everything he needs to work on the projects he has determined to work on that day.

- You will also find more information on how to set up and work on projects in the *Power Play* at the end of this chapter.

The Daily Plan

In Chapter 8: *The Super Seven Key Ingredients for Championship Living*, we will consider Priority Management in detail, and you will see the fallacy of Time Management and understand better how to live life according to your priorities. The following section on Daily Planning is only a piece of the overall Priority Management system; however, it is critical to your success as a champion.

There are more daily planners and planning systems available than can be listed in this book. In fact, to list the myriad resources would fill an entire book. I do believe, however, that it is important for you to see how one daily planning system works in order for you to understand the overall planning process for a day. Therefore, the daily planning process that we will use in this section is the system that works best for me. This just happens to be the daily planning system that works best for me. You may find that another daily planning system works better for you. The point is not necessarily which system you use, but that you find a system for daily planning and you plan each day accordingly. If you are going to live every day as a champion, as if every day were Game Day, then you must have an effective daily planning system that you use consistently.

The daily planning system that happens to work best for me is the Franklin Covey Planning System. Hyrum Smith developed this process with the associated planning sheets. In doing research, Hyrum discovered an amazing process used by Benjamin Franklin as he was following his quest to arrive at moral perfection. In his autobiography, Benjamin

Franklin wrote about a system that he developed and how he used a "little book" to track his progress.

In his "little book", Franklin recorded the areas in life that were most important to him, much like the process to develop the Life Plan. He included the goal that he wanted to achieve as well as a record of the plans that he had devised to accomplish those goals. This "little book" became a very important part of Benjamin Franklin's life. Hyrum Smith took that idea and developed from it a tool that assists people in their own daily planning process. I can't tell you how many people I have shared this process with who effectively use this tool today. The power is not in the tool, but the tool supports the power of the planning process. You can have the most powerful tool in the world, but it you don't know *how* to use it, or you *don't use* it, the results will be the same as if you never had the tool.

One component of any daily planning process should include what Franklin Covey calls *Time-Specific vs. Time-Flexible Activities.* "Time -Specific" activities are activities that must be completed or addressed within a certain time period during the day (e.g. Morning Team Meeting at 8:00 AM). Whereas "Time – Flexible" activities are activities that are not assigned a certain period of time during the day to be completed. I like to call them *Free Reign Activities.* The timing, during the day, for the completion of these *Free Reign Activities* is totally up to you.

In the two-page-per-day Franklin Covey system that I use, *Time- Specific Activities* are recorded in the "Appointment Schedule" section on the right-hand side of the left page for each day. Time-Flexible Activities, or what I call *Free Reign Activities*, are listed on the left-hand side of the left page. Franklin Covey calls this the *Prioritized Daily Task List.* (I like to call it P.D.T.L. for short.) The right page of the two-page-per-day system is reserved for daily notes. It's an ideal place to keep notes that can easily be referenced for a specific day.

The only modification I have made in my personal planning system is that I keep the Time Specific activities set aside for Building Champions coaching activities on my computer. I do this because all notes, action plans, etc. reside on that system... it's the one place I go to coach. Although this modification works well for me in coaching, I highly recommend that you follow a model that only uses one place (your planner or agenda) to plan.

The daily planning process, as taught by Franklin Covey, includes three steps as follows:

1) Check today's appointments;
2) Make a realistic list, and
3) Prioritize (ABC, 123)

Check today's appointments

Appointments or engagements are recognized as obligations to be at a certain place or do a certain thing at a certain time. When an appointment is set, barring some unforeseen hindrance, it should be kept. It's like the old saying: "Your word is your bond." Keeping appointments is a way of keeping your word. Champions keep their word, which means champions keep their appointments. These appointments require a certain amount of time for the actual appointment, along with travel time to and from the appointment. This is why careful consideration should be given to checking today's appointments so that you will know how much time you have to allocate for other requests for appointments and tasks that you would like to complete during the day.

You can also set appointments with yourself. Planning time is a prime example of an appointment that should be set and kept with yourself. This, too, is a matter of keeping your word to yourself. Have you ever heard the expression: "To thine own self be true"? Every champion knows that there should be certain times set aside to work on the projects addressed in the Business Plan as discussed above. Smart people set and keep appointments with themselves to work on specific projects. You will see more about this in Chapter 8. In coaching, we at Building Champions call this *On Time* because it is time that you are working on your business. For now, just realize that you must set and keep these appointments with yourself just as appointments are set and kept with others.

Make a realistic list

Making a realistic list refers to listing the tasks that you plan to accomplish during a given day. This list must be attainable. One can only accomplish so much during a given day, and the completion of the tasks on this list must not exceed the amount of time available for work after appointments have been kept. Too many times people try to squeeze too much into a day. This produces frustration and depression and a *pile of tasks* that are left undone. In his powerful cd set "Challenge to Succeed", Jim Rohn tells of a wonderful discovery that he found. Wealthy people have 24 hours in a day! He goes on to say, as we all know, un-wealthy people have 24 hours in a day! So what's the difference? I would say that you need to listen to the cd set to find out... and you should, but for now, it should be no surprise to you that the answer lies in what those people do with the 24 hours they have.

The key here is to track your progress in meeting appointments as well as tracking the results in accomplishing tasks. If you see that you are not allowing yourself enough time to complete tasks, you must realize that either the daily task list is too long or the appointments fill too much of the day and you must act accordingly. To act accordingly simply means that you find a way to reconcile the appointments and tasks with the number of hours in a day that you have available for business matters.

You are left with three options: 1) schedule fewer appointments; 2) assign fewer tasks to the day, or 3) create more hours in the day. Obviously no one can create more hours in the day, so options one and two are the only options that are viable. As you track your results and become more proficient in daily planning, you will have a better sense of what you actually can accomplish during the day. The next step: "Prioritize" will help you gain a better grasp on how the available time during the day needs to be invested.

Prioritize (ABC, 123)

The true power of the daily planning system that I use is that it not only allows me to record and keep track of prioritized tasks and appointments, it actually reinforces my thought process in the direction of getting things done on time and in an orderly and well thought-out manner. That well thought-out manner includes prioritizing my daily task list. By doing this I ensure that I am working on the tasks of greater importance.

The prioritization of daily tasks is a very simple process. Assign an A, B or C to each task. A's are assigned to tasks that absolutely must be done today. They are vital. B's are tasks that are important but can be rescheduled if necessary. C's are assigned to those tasks that you would like to accomplish but are truly optional. Some examples of each include:

-A: complete proposal due tomorrow
-A: call to verify tomorrow's appointment
-B: work on a project due in six weeks

-B: pick up a back-up cartridge for your computer printer
-C: begin the search process for a new laptop
-C: shop for new curtains

As you can see in these examples, it is usually very clear whether daily tasks are A's (vital), B's (important), or C's (optional). Most are dictated by the due date. The goal is to have very few A's and C's on your list. If you have a lot of A's, and they truly are A's, that should tell you that either you have over-committed or under-performed. Over-committing is saying "yes" to too many people or tasks; whereas under-performing may be an indication that procrastination is present (see Chapter 8: The Seven Key Ingredients of Championship Living for Priority Management).

You want to be scheduling and working on more B's than anything else. When B's stay on the list too long, they become A's and A's create an environment of stress and tension. Your strategy should be to invest the extra time needed right now to catch up on all of your A's and the B's that are about to become A's, then focus your daily activities on the B's with the goal, if possible, of never letting B's become A's. If you do this, you will always be working on actions or activities that are important, and seldom be forced into a state of crisis.

There is no doubt that A's will pop up from time to time for whatever reason. We don't live in a perfect world, and no one is a perfect person. The fact is, in daily planning, A's happen. However, if you follow this system and live according to the other principles in this book, you will have fewer A's slip into your daily planning process, and for the ones you do have, you will be better prepared and have more time to deal with them.

Try it and see for yourself.

In the next chapter and in Chapter 8, I will focus on helping you overcome procrastination and help you get past the trap of always getting ready to get ready.

Power Plays – Chapter 6

- Log on to www.gamedaychampions.com and follow the outlines to schedule time to complete your Life Plan, Business Vision and Business Plan (in that order).

- Life Plan: Listen to the recording of Daniel Harkavy speaking on the subject of Life Planning (follow the link in the Life Plan section of the web site).

- Business Vision: Listen to the recording of Steve Scanlon speaking on the subject of Business Vision (follow the link in the Business Vision section of the web site). Then read my article about Planting Your Vision.

- Business Planning: Listen to the Champion's Edge call for Business Planning (follow the link in the Business Planning section of the web site).

- Follow the links on the web site to complete your Life Plan, Business Vision and Business Plan. Print your Life Plan, Business Vision and Business Plan as they are completed. Begin reading your Life Plan and Business Vision every day for 90 days and then weekly thereafter. Review your Business Plan at least weekly. Do a monthly assessment concerning your success at adhering to your disciplines and staying on track with your projects.

- Find someone to be your accountability partner. If you are interested in finding a personal Life and Business Coach, follow the link to Building Champions at www. gamedaychampions.com or call us at 503-670-1013 and let us know that you are calling in response to the Power Play in this chapter.

CHAPTER 7

Implementation and the Wisdom to Get Past Getting Ready

———⎯⎯⎯⎯

A lan Jackson recorded the country-hit song *Where I Come From*. In that song, because of his accent, he was asked where he was from. He told more than just *where he came from*; he told some intriguing details about where he came from. So, I guess it's fitting to say that "where I come from" is also home to several famous performers such as Elvis Presley, Jerry Lee Lewis, and a plethora of country and contemporary Christian music artists. It has even been said that the original *Delta Dawn*, as depicted in the song, actually lived in Brownsville, Tennessee, only about thirty miles from where I call home. There's no doubt that this area is rich in folklore, performers and songwriters.

One performer / songwriter who lived "where I come from" was Carl Perkins. He wrote the classic *Blue Suede Shoes* made famous by Elvis Presley. As you may know, that song starts out as follows: "Well it's one for the money, two for the show, three to get ready, now go, cat, go…" Sadly, too many people stop at the "three to get ready" mark. They never get to the "go, cat, go" part; they never get past getting ready.

On my dad's 70th birthday I wanted to do something different than just giving him another shirt or tie; I wanted to do something that he would remember. Suddenly I realized that, although we have always lived within seventy-five miles of Memphis, that my dad had never visited Graceland (famed home of Elvis Presley). People from all over the world fly into Memphis just to visit Graceland. My mom and dad had never been! So I called my mom and told her about my "crazy" idea to take them to Graceland.

Mom jumped right on the idea and said, "Let's go!" We only disclosed to dad that we were taking him to Memphis to eat. By the time we got to Memphis, my dad was asleep so we were able to "sneak" up on Graceland without him knowing what we were doing. A stone wall to keep away intruders lines the Graceland property; on that wall is graffiti with notes from fans from all over the world. We were able to park along side that wall. When I woke dad up he was surprised to see that we were at the gates of Graceland. It was a pleasant surprise.

While on the tour we were able to see where Elvis lived, along with his gold records and other memorabilia. Since this was my second time through the mansion and surrounding grounds, I took a lot of time to watch my mom and dad's expressions as they took their first tour. However, there was something that caught me by surprise that I didn't remember from my first tour. It was something that made me realize the stark difference between *Getting Ready* and *Implementation*. There was a recording of Priscilla Presley (Elvis' ex-wife) talking about being with Elvis backstage and watching him walk out on stage for each performance.

She recalled that just before the concert, only moments before he walked on stage, everything seemed normal to her... she was just with her husband as he was about to leave for work; but when the music started, and Elvis took the first few steps toward the audience, she said that she would get goose bumps and feel the excitement as if it were the first time she had ever seen him perform. Elvis getting ready for the performance was business as usual, while implementation (or Elvis walking on stage with the music playing) changed everything! When you walk on stage and start to implement, you have the opportunity to change everything.

In this chapter we will focus on *getting past getting ready*. We will focus on taking those first few steps to walk out onto the stage of your life where your performance actually begins. We will focus on implementation. Throughout this book we have discussed desire, potential, courage, vision and preparation. Now it's time to make something happen. It's time to expose that desire, reach for that potential, put that courage to work and bring that vision to fruition. It's time for implementation!

The word "implementation" is the action derivative of the word "implement" which, according to *Webster's American Dictionary* means: "to carry out or put into effect." Another word that could be used interchangeably with *implement* is *execute,* from which we get the word *executive.* Champions understand that they have to consider themselves to be the Chief Executive Officer (CEO) of their own affairs in order to insure that what needs to get done actually does get done. They understand that they have to take 100% responsibility for whatever does or does not get done as it pertains to their quest for excellence. Although much has been written about accepting total responsibility, champions know that being responsible is a fundamental building block in the world of successful people.

Living in an Upside Down World

Let's look back at the words of that classic song, *Blue Suede Shoes,* to see just how upside-down or backwards so many people are when it comes to success. Look at the order: "One for the money," "Two for the show," "Three to get ready", then "Go, cat, go!" Shouldn't it really go something more like this: "One: Get ready; "Two: Go, cat, go,"; then comes "Three: "The Show", and finally, "The Money.""? I know that was hard to read; it probably even sounds convoluted and it doesn't fit in the song, but that's the way things really work.

Too many people act like the "Go, cat, go" part comes after "The Show" and "The Money" when, in fact, "The Show", or whatever we do for a living, comes before "The Money" is handed out. So many people today have a "Show me the money" first, or entitlement mentality. That's not the case with champions. They understand that if they want to see the money, the show comes first... and that show better be good.

Let's look at another example – Hollywood. The famous phrase in Hollywood is "Lights – Camera – Action!" in that order. But isn't that really out of order as it pertains to the way things really work in life? In reality, first comes the "Action" (something significant is accomplished), then the "Lights" are turned on for others to get a much clearer view of what is happening, and then the "Camera" appears because there is enough interest that warrants the action to be recorded. So although "Action – Lights - Camera" doesn't easily roll off the tongue like "Lights – Camera – Action", champions understand that it is the order of success.

A Call to Action

So this is it, this is where dreams either die or grow and thrive. Without action, the grandest of all dreams is wasted away. In his best- selling book, *The Traveler's Gift*, author Andy Andrews' character David Ponder was led by his angelic guide Gabriel into a room full of ideas, projects, pictures, schematics of cures for diseases, and inventions of every kind. Upon quizzing Gabriel, David Ponder was astonished that Gabriel was giving him a tour of "The Land That Never Was"! None of the ideas or projects had been completed. The pictures he saw in that room were pictures of people never given the chance to be born. The cure for pancreatic, liver, or colon cancer lay dormant on paper that was never completed. The inventions never made it to market because they never left the drawing board... they were never acted upon. When David asked Gabriel why people quit, Gabriel's response was: "As a human, you detour and ease off because you lack understanding. You quit because you lack faith." He was telling David that we quit by failing to take action; we fail to take action because of lack of understanding and lack of faith.

Recently I was fortunate enough to have some time with Andy at an event in Palm Desert, CA. During that time I wanted to garner some wisdom from such a gifted writer as Andy Andrews. If you haven't read one (or all) of his books, you are missing out on one of the finest authors of our time. In his book, *Island of Saints* you will find a cliff-hanging story of forgiveness; in *The Lost Choice* you can read a gripping story about the power of our daily choices in life, and in *The Traveler's Gift* you will be mesmerized by stories of "seven decisions that determine personal success."

As you might imagine, I was determined to hang on to every word Andy said after I struck up a conversation with him about writing. I wasn't disappointed. He gave me one nugget of advice that I didn't expect, but that nugget has proved to be immensely valuable during the writing of this book. His words still ring in my ears. Andy Andrews looked right at me and said: "Writing is work. Don't wait to be inspired. Just sit down and write; the inspiration will come. Just write." I can't tell you how many times I thought about what he said as I was writing this book. There were many times that I didn't feel inspired, and didn't even feel like writing, when I heard Andy's words: "Just write". Many times my mind went back to that room in *The Traveler's Gift* where Gabriel showed David Ponder the things that never were in the land that never was. There was no way that I was going to let *Every Day is Game Day* find its way to the land that never was. Although, had I not followed Andy's advice and kept writing, that's exactly where this book would be today. I would still be waiting for inspiration to write, and you wouldn't be reading. There would be no Power Plays for you to implement at the end of each chapter.

What about you? What do you need to write? What is it that you need to be doing? What ideas or plans do you have that are headed toward the land that never was? I can promise you that it's easier than you think to allow ideas and projects that you have to land in that dreadful place. Just today, as I was going about my business, I thought of an idea for another book. All I can tell you at this point is that, at least in my opinion, it was an awesome idea. However, I can't tell you what the idea was because I failed to take action on it by writing it in my journal. In my mind, it was such an awesome idea that I thought I wouldn't forget it. I forgot it. Philosopher Jim Rohn has told the story many times that his dad taught him not to trust his own memory. He taught him to journal those ideas and thoughts. (Jim Rohn has a wonderful resource on journaling… it's a cd titled "How to Journal" – See the Power Play at the end of this chapter for more information.) Sometimes we miss opportunities forever if we don't take immediate action. Sometimes that action is as simple as jotting a note in a journal or, as John Maxwell calls it, writing it down in your *Thinking Companion*.

The Next Steps

Capturing the idea for action and then planning for that action is absolutely essential to getting things done. However, there is more that is required if you want to reach fruition of your vision. I am a "people watcher" and, at least for me, it's fun to just think about why people are doing what they are doing and whether that action is either helping or hindering them from living their dreams.

A couple of days ago, after working out at the gym with my son and a fellow coach, I realized that I had left something in my locker. My son and I drove back to the gym and he went in to get it for me. As I was waiting for him to come back, I had an epiphany as I watched people come and go from the gym. Some looked as though they actually lived in the gym (or at least lived for going to the gym), whereas others appeared as though they were walking into the gym for the first time. In other words, some looked as though they were in great shape while others seemed to have more shape than they needed.

The thought occurred to me that while some were just getting started, others were already gym rats. Some had been disciplined over a long period of time while others were just beginning the journey. However there is more to that picture than meets the eye. There were some, of course, that although they didn't look as though they were in great shape, had actually been members of the gym for years. They just hadn't disciplined themselves to be regular in their work-outs. Some make it to the gym but seem to be there for more of a fashion statement than for the workout. In my opinion, if you aren't sweating, you aren't working out... you might as well just be there for the show, and some are. Getting ready to go to the gym does nothing for you, just as going to the gym but not really working out has no real and lasting value. There must be a plan and the discipline to follow it.

If you work out regularly at a public gym you know that there are certain months that are more crowded than others. For example, January is usually horrible while May and June are much better. You see, there is a group of people who join gyms as a result of a New Year's Resolution. Most of them never make it past February or March. An acquaintance, who at one time managed a gym in New York, told me that proprietors of health clubs often refer to these people as *resolutionists*. They join the health club in January and by March they are gone... although they are still paying the monthly bill. He went on to say that January isn't the only month that brings in the *short- timers*. He told me that mid-spring brings another wave of people. These are, for the most part, people who sign up because they want to look better at the pool during the summer. Again, for the most part, these people are here today and gone tomorrow. Mid to late fall brings another group of short-timers; these are people who join because they want to look better for the holidays. Again, they are here today and gone tomorrow.

The one constant that I have noticed about everyone who comes to the gym is that they are there for a reason. There is something that brings them in and causes them to sign a contract that will require them to pay, whether or not they ever enter the doors of the gym again. They all want something. The cold hard truth is that some get what they want and some don't. The ones who do get what they want are the ones who join and stick with it. Those are the ones who come to the gym and get a good workout in whether they really want to go to the gym that day or not. They are the ones who get past getting ready. As the famous philosopher, Larry the Cable Guy, says: They get in there and *Git –R-Done.*

The Art of Taking Action

In Three Easy Steps

There are three basic steps in the art of getting past getting ready and taking specific and strategic action. These three steps will allow you to have the opportunity to bask in the fruition of your vision. According to *Webster's American Dictionary* "art" can be defined as an ability to make or do something (a practical skill). These practical skills for taking action are simply as follows:

1) Get Ready
2) Get Set
3) Go

Step 1: Get Ready

Although this was addressed in "Chapter 6: Champions Prepare to Win", we are reviewing this because it is mission-critical that you actually "get ready." Getting ready includes planning – or preparing. There is just no getting past this step. Jim Rohn once stated that if you don't have a plan, you will most likely be part of someone else's plan. In that case, I wonder what their plan for you would be... I would venture to guess that your role in their plan would probably be of more benefit to them than to you. Although there are far too many people who never take action, there are also far too many people who take action without planning. They may seem to be ahead of the game in the early stages, but this always backfires. You must always get ready first. Acting without planning is like shooting without taking aim.

Getting ready is extremely important. Throughout any process there are multiple points in time when one must "get ready". This doesn't just occur at the beginning. It occurs several times because processes and projects alike are simply made up of multiple steps. You must "get ready" for each step. If you are not ready, then you can never "get set" and if you aren't set, you certainly don't need to proceed or "go". However, for a process or project to be brought to fruition, all three steps must be present. Let's consider the next step, "Get Set."

Step 2: Get Set

If you have ever watched a sprinter "get set" for a race, you probably know that person can either win or lose races because of (or the lack of) that short burst of speed when the starter's pistol is fired. They get in that crouched position so they can use their leg muscles to thrust them into a fast start. It's the same for other athletes, from swimmers to football players. The basic principles of "getting" set must be followed in order for that particular athlete to be ready for the "go" signal, whether that signal is the sound of a starter's pistol firing or the snapping of a football from the center to the quarterback. That's it. It's not for looks; it's for maximum speed and power from the very start.

Getting set, in terms of becoming or remaining a champion, has to do with the process of making sure everything is in place for you to succeed in your endeavor. If this part is skipped, if you go straight from "Get Ready" to "Go", chances are that details will fall through the cracks. Something that needs to be done will not get done.

There is a subtle, yet distinct difference between "Get Ready" and "Get Set". The best way I can describe this difference is to share with you a story that happened to me, as I was about to interview for a job about twelve years ago. I had always been interested in the field of human resources; although I was already working in the HR department, I wanted to obtain the position of human resource manager for some company. However, I had no experience as a human resource manager. So the first thing I had to do was to get ready.

Getting ready meant that I needed to develop a plan to do everything I could to enhance my chances of landing that position when the opportunity presented itself. I did just that. Since I had already obtained my degree in Management from the University of Mississippi, I felt that I had the formal education piece of the equation under my belt. However, there were other things I could do to "get ready". So I put the plan together and began to act upon that plan. I guess you could say from a micro point of view of the goal I "Got Ready", "Got Set" and "Acted on Go" in the process of getting ready for the opportunity to become a human resource manager.

The first thing I did was to join the local chapter of The Society of Human resource Management. I became active in the chapter and soon became vice president and eventually president of the chapter. I also went through the process of becoming certified through the national organization. This really helped in the area of credentials since I was only the second person within a three-county radius to be certified. The only other person had been certified through a grandfather clause. So I was actually the first in that three county radius to pass the exam. This was the process of "Getting Ready." I could "get ready" for the opportunity to interview, but previous to this, I could not "get set" for a specific interview because I didn't know which company would give me the opportunity first.

On a certain day at a certain time I received a call from a local human resource manager who was about to be promoted. He wanted me to interview for the position of assistant human resource manager so I could learn the ropes of that company under his tutelage and then assume his position within a two- to three- year period of time. He invited me to have lunch with him and we discussed the next steps of the selection process. At this point I was "ready" and it was time to "get set". Getting set is specific to the race at hand. Just as a runner can have practice runs on several different tracks, the "getting set" part only happens on the specified track on the specified race day. It was race day for me, and I knew the track upon which I was about to run.

The next steps of the hiring process included interviews with three people at the corporate level. I had done all I needed to do to "get ready"; I was ready to assume the position. "Getting set," meant that I had to be mentally prepared for this specific interview. I had to be in that crouched position to use whatever muscles or resources necessary to give me that initial burst of power and speed in the interview; just as a sprinter, after all those days of practice, gets set in the position to run.

I prepared mentally by doing some extensive research on the company conducting the interview. To the extent that I could find information, I knew that company inside and out. I was mentally prepared and the interview day was set. That day came and I found myself walking through the process with ease. I had done what I needed to do to "get ready" and then I did what I needed to do to "get set". I was ready to "go" and everything went well that day.

In fact, the interview process went so well that, rather than interviewing with three people, I interviewed with seven (the seventh person being from the organization that actually owned the company). I guess you could say that I interviewed with corporate's *corporate person*. It was then that the question came that I was neither ready, nor set to answer.

This person asked me if I had been wondering what was going on since I had interviewed with more than twice the number of people that I was originally told that I would be speaking with that day. Of course I said, "Yes." He proceeded to tell me that all of the people with whom I had spoken that day had been very impressed and that during the course of the day, they had actually started interviewing me for a different position. This position was in the corporate office. He asked me if I would be willing to move to their corporate offices for this position. Since I was neither ready, nor set to answer that question I gave a quick answer that I subsequently regretted. I respectfully said "no".

Without telling me what the position was, he told me that he understood the reasons that I had given for saying no and that he appreciated my coming in that day. That was it. I never heard another word from them. Some time later the human resource manager that had originally given me the opportunity called and asked me what happened during the process. He said that I had really impressed the people I interviewed with that day and he was wondering what I had done to do so well. At that point I basically told him what I had done to "get set" for the interviews (obviously he already knew what I had done to "get ready" since he was the first one to give me the opportunity to interview for the assistant manager's position).

The moral to that story is that when you take time to "Get Ready" and "Get Set", you put yourself in a position to excel far beyond what you could do if you are neither ready nor set. That's obvious by my response to one question that I was neither ready nor set to answer. I was ready and set for the interview with the original three interviewers, so much so that I was able to hold that momentum through four more interviews right up until the end.

As a champion (or aspiring champion) in life and business you have to do what is necessary to "get ready" and then "get set" for whatever it takes to fulfill your goals and live out your vision. You cannot by-pass these two vital steps in the process; to do so could spell disaster.

Step 3: Go

This is the step that usually either gets procrastinated and remains undone, or gets done without the added value of the first two steps. The "Go" step is the step where the desired end-results are either welcomed or found wanting.

There is so much that goes on during the "Go" step that can either make or break the outcome. It is in this step where champions often rely on muscle memory to help them see the achievements they want. Too many times people jump to the "Go" step without getting ready or getting set, and they find that there is no muscle memory to carry them on.

Let's look at a couple of examples. The other day, after a workout at the gym, I decided to swim in the pool with my daughter. Although we played more than we swam, we did try to swim some laps. Actually "laps" being plural doesn't describe what we did that day. We tried to swim one lap (it's a rather large pool and I hadn't been swimming in almost a year… it was right after working out). Needless to say, I didn't make it a full lap. However, that was okay since we were the only ones in the pool and no one, other than my wife who was sitting at a table beside the pool, could see that I didn't even make one full lap. After all, my goal wasn't to be a distance swimmer and my planned workout didn't include swimming.

Just as we were about to move away from the lap area, an individual who didn't seem to be in much better shape entered the pool and began to swim laps. That's right, laps… as in plural. He swam and swam… lap after lap until I actually got tired watching. When he was finished I asked him how far he swam. He said that it was only a half-mile that day because that was the first time he had been in the pool this year. But wait, that was my excuse. I had justified the fact that I didn't make it for a complete lap because I hadn't been swimming in almost a year. However, there was a difference between him and me.

He said he had been an aquatics instructor the year before, and had been swimming a mile at a time. He added that he was in the process of working his way back up to a mile. He was "getting ready", so that he could come back and get into position, or "get set" to "go" a mile. He had the muscle memory to start the process further down the line than I did. His "Get Ready" and "Get Set" were different than mine.

Then, another individual entered the pool area and immediately went head first into the pool (at the shallow end) and proceeded to swim one lap. After that lap he got out of the pool, toweled off and went back into the gym. Immediately, the guy who had just finished swimming the half-mile looked at my daughter and said: "Did you see what that guy just did?" He continued: "Don't ever do that. Don't ever dive in the shallow end; you could break your neck." I had just witnessed two beautiful illustrations of the *Get Ready. Get Set. Go!* principles. You have to "get ready" and "get set" appropriately before you ever "go" accomplish your goal.

The Science of Taking Action

Although discipline is the key to taking action, the process of taking action itself includes 4 elements of science. According to Webster's American Dictionary, one part of the definition of science is that science is "skill based upon training." The four elements we will discuss in this section are examples of skills that are based upon training. In other words, these steps can, and should be learned. The scientific steps of taking action are:

1) Timing;
2) Development of and Adherence to Systems and Processes;

3) Tracking, and
4) Accountability
The Science of Timing

You may have heard that timing is everything. Well, it may not be *everything*, but it plays a starring role in our activities. In the Bible, in Ecclesiastes 3:1-8 (NKJV), Solomon wrote:

> *To everything there is a season,*
> *A time for every purpose under heaven:*
> *A time to be born*
> *And a time to die;*
> *A time to plant*
> *And a time to pluck what is planted;*
> *A time to kill,*
> *And a time to heal;*
> *A time to break down;*
> *And a time to build up;*
> *A time to weep,*
> *And a time to laugh;*
> *A time to mourn,*
> *And a time to dance;*
> *A time to cast away stones,*
> *And a time to gather stones;*
> *A time to embrace,*
> *And a time to refrain from embracing;*
> *A time to gain,*
> *And a time to lose;*
> *A time to keep,*
> *And a time to throw away;*
> *A time to tear,*
> *And a time to sew;*
> *A time to keep silence,*
> *And a time to speak;*

> *A time to love,*
> *And a time to hate;*
> *A time of war,*
> *And a time of peace.*

So if the wisest man who ever lived said there is a time for all things, wouldn't you think that the timing of actions taken is important? There are natural laws that govern many of the *time to's* that you just read. Likewise, there are natural laws that govern when action must be taken in everything we do. For example, the best time to plant an oak tree was thirty years ago; but if you haven't planted that oak tree yet, the second best time to plant an oak tree is today. As you should know by now... **Every Day is Game Day!** Champions understand the natural laws that govern when they should take action and they respond accordingly.

The Science of Development of and Adherence to Systems and Processes

Systems and processes act as guardrails. They provide the structure necessary to complete a task as effectively and efficiently as possible. To illustrate, there is a story of two lumberjacks cutting down trees in a forest. During the first few days they are fairly proficient at what they do, but after a few days they become less and less effective in cutting down trees. One day a person passing by asked why they are less effective and seem to be working so hard to cut the trees. The reply from the lumberjacks was that the saw had become dull. Immediately the person passing by asked why they haven't sharpened the saw. To this, the lumberjacks replied that they didn't have time to sharpen the saw; they were too busy cutting down trees!

Again, Solomon addresses this principle when in Ecclesiastes 10:10 he says: "If the ax is dull, and one does not sharpen the edge, then he must use more strength; but wisdom brings success." In this case, wisdom refers to the principle of developing and adhering to a system or process (i.e. sharpening the ax) that will lend itself to greater success. Champions understand this principle. They develop and adhere to systems and processes that will help them be both efficient and effective in their efforts. Daniel Harkavy clearly addresses this principle in his landmark book *Becoming A Coaching Leader.* It's called working smart.

The Science of Tracking

In "Chapter 5: Champions Practice 4-Dimensional Vision", we discussed the third dimension of vision as being Display (the scoreboard or tracking process). Although there is no need to rehash that material here, there is a need for understanding the importance of this step in the implementation stage. You may have heard that what gets measured gets improved. In many cases, that is an understatement. Consider this: how fast would you drive if you absolutely knew beyond a shadow of a doubt that your speed would never be tracked by a law enforcement officer? The answer to that is probably faster than you currently drive. In many cases, it's not the speed limit that makes you drive slower. It's the thought of being measured (or caught). We will discuss the enforcement piece next.

Champions know that they need to develop a method of tracking the vital result areas in life and business. They understand what Solomon meant in Proverbs 27:23 (NKJV) when he admonished that we should "Be diligent to know the state of your flocks, and attend to your herds." Obviously most of us don't have flocks or herds, but I believe that he was instructing us to track and understand the state of our affairs. Champions are diligent in this regard.

The Science of Accountability

To whom are you accountable? Champions understand that they must set up relationships with accountability partners in order to consistently follow through with the action process. Some people say they are accountable to themselves. I partially understand that thought process when coupled with Shakespeare's statement: "To thine own self be true," but I can't endorse this philosophy as it relates to accountability.

If I were to ask you if you had ever just neglected a discipline or something that you knew you needed to do, I presume that you would say, "Yes." Did it hurt you? Did you have to pay for it later? Have you ever been caught speeding and had to pay a fine? Surely most, if not all of us, would have to raise our hands in shame and admit that we have. Wouldn't it be easier to stay on track if we just had someone we trusted who cares enough about us to hold us accountable?

Jim Rohn addresses this topic in his book *Leading an Inspired Life*. He says: "Failure is not a cataclysmic event. It is not the result of one major incident, but rather of a long list of accumulated little failings." He goes on to say: "The danger is looking at an undisciplined day and concluding that no great harm has been done... repeating today's small failures can easily turn your life into a major disaster. Success, on the other hand, is just the same process in reverse." You see, champions understand that although accountability isn't fun, it is necessary to help them avoid those "small failures" and "undisciplined days." After all, they know if they are going to do what they need to do anyway, that additional accountability won't impede them; however, if they have a tendency to slide, it could save them. Champions do whatever is needed to stay on top of their game every day because "Every Day is Game Day"!

If you are ready to take on accountability as recommended in the Power Play at the end of this chapter, you are ready for *The Super Seven Ingredients of Championship Living* that you will find waiting for you in the next chapter.

Power Plays – Chapter 7

- Listen to Jim Rohn's recording: *How to Journal* - you will find a link to purchase this recording at www.gamedaychampions.com

- Make a list of systems and processes needed to provide the structure to help you follow the plans you developed at the end of Chapter 6.

- Determine how you will track the vital result areas in your life and business. (If necessary, re-read the "Display" section of the "4 Dimensional Vision Process" in Chapter 5.)

- Read *Becoming A Coaching Leader* by Daniel Harkavy – see the BACL link at www.gamedaychampions.com (You may be ready to take the challenge to become a certified coach through Building Champions.)

- Begin to read *Leading An Inspired Life* by Jim Rohn - a link to this book may be found at www.gamedaychampions.com

CHAPTER 8

The Super Seven Ingredients of Championship Living

⎯⎯⎯∞∞∞⎯⎯⎯

No one is actually born a champion. I have never heard a doctor or nurse proudly announce to anyone that they are parents of a new baby boy or girl champion. Sure, some people have natural talent to excel in certain fields, but with history on the side of this argument, not everyone who has natural talent is a champion, neither are those lacking a plethora of natural talent excluded from being champions. There is hope for us! People develop into champions over time, and there are certain active ingredients or learned behaviors that are found in champions.

In this chapter we will explore what I believe to be the seven most common ingredients (characteristics) found in champions. By chapter's end you will not only know the ingredients, you will be able to use them together with your Life Plan, Business Vision, and Business Plan to take you further down the road to becoming a champion than you have ever been before. If there is a shopping list for championship living, this is it:

The Super Seven Ingredients of Championship Living

#1 Champions have a winning attitude
#2 Champions seek wisdom and knowledge
#3 Champions consistently implement with excellence
#4 Champions employ priority management every day
#5 Champions seek accountability
#6 Champions embrace the team concept
#7 Champions continually develop self-discipline

Championship Living Ingredient #1
Champions have a winning attitude

There has been so much written about "attitude" that I almost didn't include it in this list because I didn't want to be redundant. Still, there is no way that I could write about the ingredients of Championship Living without addressing *attitude.* It's like trying to bake a cake without including the cake mix; the eggs and oil just don't make for an exciting dessert without the cake mix. Not only do I know that attitude must be included in the list, it must be number one! Having an appropriate attitude, the attitude of a champion, is the most important ingredient in championship living. In the game of life, attitude is the overriding ingredient that sets the stage for winning or losing. The best example I can think of is found in a story I call *The Best Hire in College Football.*

The Best Hire in College Football

The University of Southern California is an incredible school known for very successful graduates. Founded in

1880 in Los Angeles, a small frontier town, with 53 students and 10 teachers, USC has become a world-class research university with an enrollment of 33,000 students. Today it is the oldest private research university in the West, although, world-class academics isn't the only thing going on in what is affectionately known as Troy. The USC Trojan football team is the focus on Saturday afternoons during autumn months. USC enjoys one of the richest college football programs in the nation, boasting more than 10 national championships. However, there have been some lean years. From 1996 through the 2000 season, the not so mighty Trojans won 31 and lost 29.

The Trojans were hardly what anyone would call a *powerhouse* in college football. Enter Pete Carroll, an experienced NFL coach hired after the 2000 season that brought a new fire and attitude to Troy. From his first season in 2001 through the next five years, the Trojans won 54 and only lost 10 games while winning two national championships.

What was the difference in the five years before and after Pete Carroll's arrival? What did Pete Carroll do in the middle of that 10-year span that made the difference? It started with a winning attitude, but it didn't end there. It takes time to develop a winning attitude on a team. Pete's first season record didn't look much different than the previous five years; but what cannot be seen in the record books could be seen on the field. They won more games in the second half of the season than they did in the first half.

Pete Carroll brought a different attitude to the team and when the team adopted that attitude, they started developing the other six ingredients of championship living. It all started with attitude, it always does; but attitude alone doesn't make you a champion. It only prepares you to appropriately apply the next six ingredients. If your attitude is where it should be, read on. You are ready to apply the next six ingredients.

Championship Ingredient #2
Champions continually seek wisdom and knowledge

The wisest man to ever live on this earth was King Solomon. Imagine this. What would you do if you heard a deep strong voice coming from the sky that said, "Ask! What shall I give you?" Suppose that you knew beyond a shadow of a doubt that the voice you heard was the voice of God Almighty! What would you ask for? Although it would be fun to play with that thought, it actually happened to Solomon.

Solomon was the son of King David, the one who killed the giant Goliath. At the time he was about to be named king, not only did he have the big shoes of his father to fill, he had to do it at an early age. During the final days of his life, King David said the following words to his son Solomon: "I go the way of all the earth; be strong, therefore, and prove yourself as a man."

Wow! Just think about the gravity of those words. When he said "I go the way of all the earth", David was referring to the fact that his life was ending, and he wanted his son to be prepared to take over as king and lead the nation. "Be strong therefore, and prove yourself a man" carried with it the connotation that he (David) had done all he could do to prepare Solomon to be king, and that it was now time for Solomon to stand up like a man, be strong, and prove himself worthy.

That's when it happened. After David's death, Solomon sat on the throne of his father David. One night while at Gibeon, God appeared to Solomon in a dream. It was then that Solomon was given the gift of a lifetime! God said: "Ask! What shall I give you?"

It was Solomon's response that shaped the future of his reign as king. Solomon said: "You have shown great mercy to Your servant David, my father, because he walked before

You in truth, in righteousness, and in uprightness of heart with You... You have chosen, a great people, too numerous to be numbered or counted. Therefore give to Your servant an understanding heart to judge Your people, that I may discern between good and evil. For who is able to judge this great people of Yours?"

God's reply to Solomon was just as amazing. He was pleased with what came from Solomon's heart and said: "Because you have asked this thing, and have not asked long life for yourself, nor have you asked riches for yourself, nor have asked the life of your enemies, but have asked for yourself understanding to discern justice, behold, I have done according to your words; see, I have given you a wise and understanding heart, so that there has not been anyone like you before you, nor shall any like you arise after you. And I have also given you what you have not asked: both riches and honor, so that there shall not be anyone like you among the kings all your days. So if you walk in My ways, to keep My statutes and My commandments, as your father David walked, then I will lengthen your days."

The end-result of gaining and applying wisdom is always much better than what was expected at the outset of the quest for wisdom. The payoff for wisdom is always HUGE! According to Webster's Dictionary, wisdom is defined as "the ability to discern inner qualities and relationship (insight)... good sense (judgment)... and a wise attitude or course of action."

With wisdom, you can see what others can't; you understand the inner workings and related parts and know the appropriate course of action to take.

Wisdom has to do with an understanding that goes beyond the mere knowledge of facts. English poet Lord Alfred Tennyson once said: "Knowledge comes, but wisdom lingers." Wisdom is the ability to know what to do, how to do it, and when. Rudyard Kipling, a Nobel Prize winning short-story writer, novelist and poet remarked that he keeps six honest serving-men that taught him all he knew; their names were What, Why, When, How, Where and Who. Champions have the same six honest serving-men because champions continually seek wisdom.

Although knowledge comes and wisdom lingers, this in no way diminishes the need for knowledge. Francis Bacon coined the phrase, "Knowledge itself is power." In reality, wisdom is the understanding of how to properly use knowledge. There is no substitute for gaining knowledge and champions know this.

Champions have a Knowledge Acquisition Plan. They know what they need to learn. They have a plan to grow in knowledge. As a life and business coach I have made the commitment to myself, as well as to my clients that I will continually be dedicated to life- long learning. One reason is that if I weren't continually learning, I could possibly coast along and be an effective coach for a period of time, but that wouldn't last. In order for me to continue to dispense value in coaching sessions, it is imperative for me to fill my own *knowledge tank* first.

I was told in high school that if I would sleep the night before a test with my textbook under my pillow, the knowledge would enter my mind via osmosis. That, of course, didn't work… it just made my head uncomfortable on my pillow. The only way I can gain knowledge is to ardently seek it. There is no secret formula. It takes work that quickly reaps rich rewards.

Champions continually seek wisdom and knowledge because they know that wisdom and knowledge are keys to success. However, although one may be very knowledgeable and wise, if that wisdom or knowledge is not put to use, they are non-factors. This brings us to the third ingredient of championship living.

Championship Living Ingredient #3
Champions consistently implement with excellence

Now we are getting to the nuts and bolts of what to do to live like a champion. You can fully know your purpose, be clear about your vision, and be full of wisdom and knowledge; but if you do nothing about it, nothing will happen. In their marvelous book, *Execution: The Discipline of Getting Things Done,* Larry Bossidy and Ram Charan so eloquently state that: "In its most fundamental sense, execution is a systematic way of exposing reality and acting on it."

The most important thing to know after the vision has been written down is exactly what to act on. I coach my clients to develop a list of gaps between their visions, for life or business, and current reality in each area. After compiling the list, it's easier to target areas that need attention if the vision is going to be fulfilled. At that point my clients can prioritize the list and begin to develop a plan to implement. A prioritized action list allows them to know that they are executing the actions that will result in big payoffs.

There are a lot of reasons why people fail to implement consistently. Some are:

1) Fear of Failure:

There are times people are afraid to try because they are afraid to fail. The fear of failure can be crippling to any vision. Many people fail to see that failure can be their friend.

2)Fear of Success:

Believe it or not, some people fear success because they aren't sure they will know what to do with success after they achieve it. They know what they want, but are not sure what they will do when they actually get it.

3) Procrastination:

My definition of procrastination is as follows: *Procrastination is the space in time between inspiration and implementation.* Think about it. Once you are inspired to do something, the space in time between when you are inspired and when you actually act is a representation of procrastination. People procrastinate because they aren't sure what to do next (they don't have a well thought-out plan). At other times, people procrastinate because they are waiting for the stars to be aligned and everything to be "just right" before they start. This can be a killer for any vision, since there is rarely an occasion when "everything" is "just right". One problem with procrastination is that after a period of procrastination, the law of diminishing intent takes root and the procrastinator loses the resolve to reach a goal.

4) Laziness:

Sometimes people don't implement consistently because they are lazy. They are *dreamers* and that's all they may ever be! These people are **not** champions.

I am reminded of a story I once heard about three lazy men lying in an alley. On a certain day a well-dressed man walked down the alley where the men were lying and promptly told them that he would give $1,000 dollars in 10 crisp $100 dollar bills to the one who could prove he was the laziest of the three. Immediately two of the three men jumped into action and tried to convince the man with the offer that each was the laziest one of them all. However, upon noticing the one man still lying against the wall in the alley, the man walked over to the seemingly unimpressed alley dweller and repeated his offer and concluded with an emphatic, "Don't you want to prove you are the laziest and get the money?" Without moving another muscle, the man opened his eyes, looked up at the man with the money and said: "Just put it in my pocket."

Although you may not know anyone that lazy, I am confident that you have seen others who allow at least a little bit of laziness to prevent them from achieving their goals. Since you've read this far I am confident that this does not describe you, you are a champion (at least in-the-making), and champions are not lazy.

5) They don't feel like implementing:

I could have associated this reason for not implementing with laziness. I chose not to because there very well could be some physiological or physical factors playing a role in the "feeling". If this is the case, I would suggest that the person consult with a medical caregiver to better understand the problem at hand and develop a course of action to overcome it.

Still, there are times when champions don't *feel* like doing something, and yet they get up and do it anyway. The best example of this that I know is that of Jordan Rubin. Jordan was an athlete at Florida State University who suddenly became deathly ill.

The story that ensued after he became ill is one of the best inspirational stories of all time. He decided to fight his illness like a true champion. He was on a mission! He did what he didn't feel like doing so that he could live his vision and complete his mission. He fought, and in his book *The Great Physician's Rx for Health* you will find how he overcame the following:

- Chronic candidacies (or yeast overgrowth);
- Entamoeba histolytica, a parasite that causes amebic dysentery;
- Cryptosporidiosis, a protozoan infection that causes severe intestinal illness;

- Incipient diabetes;
- Jaundice;
- Insomnia;
- Hair loss;
- Endocarditis, a heart infection;
- Eye inflammation;
- Prostate and bladder infections;
- Extreme anemia;
- Chronic electrolyte imbalance;
- Elevated C-reactive protein;
- Chronic fatigue;
- Arthritis;
- Leukocytosis, an abnormal increase in white blood cells, and
- Malabsorption syndrome, his body was unable to absorb sufficient nutrients from food

Jordan Rubin not only fought against all of these medical issues going on within his body, he fought them all at the same time... and won! If anybody had reasons to give up and quit it was Jordan, and he had many; but he didn't, he fought through it so that he could live his mission. Today he is doing just that! He is the founder of Garden of Life, a health and wellness company. He holds earned doctoral degrees in naturopathic medicine, nutrition, and natural therapies. He is the author of three books and has appeared on more than 300 television and radio programs and has written several articles on nutrition. He is a husband, and father, and is living his vision to the fullest! Jordan Rubin didn't feel like it... but he did it anyway. Champions consistently implement with excellence. Jordan Rubin consistently implements with excellence. Jordan Rubin is a champion in the truest sense of the word!

Championship Living Ingredient #4
Champions Employ Priority Management Every Day

Time Management is an Oxymoron is the title of one of the first articles I ever wrote in the area of Priority Management. In that article, I discussed the fact that you can't manage time any more effectively than you can manage the weather or traffic. Time Management is a term that is misnamed. So what can you do with time? The answer can be likened to the weather or traffic; you adjust. If it's raining, you dress differently; if the traffic is congested, you may take a different route. Although you can't manage the weather or the traffic, you can manage yourself and your response to the weather or traffic.

That's what Priority Management is all about. Although you can't manage time, you can very well manage yourself around priorities. You manage yourself around priorities that you have pre-set such as your Life Plan and your Business Plan. Priority Management is something that is entirely under your control. You set the priorities, and you manage yourself around those priorities. The time will take care of itself.

If you have ever listened to the song *Fly Like an Eagle*, you will remember the lyrics: "Time keeps on ticking, ticking, ticking into the future." At another point in the song you will hear: "Time keeps on slipping, slipping, slipping into the future." All that means is that you can't stop time, pause it, speed it up, or slow it down. It just keeps on ticking, ticking, ticking… and slipping, slipping, slipping away into the future. You have no control over what time does; you only have control over what you do with the time you have.

What you do with your time determines what type of return you get for the time you invested. That's how I like to think about time. Over the past several years I have determined that I will not use the term "spend time" as in, "Let's spend some time together." Instead, I say, "Let's invest time with each other." This indicates a shift in perspective that communicates how I value time. When I say *spend* I am not thinking so much about getting a return; but when I say *invest* I think more about what I will gain in return for the time I have given to an activity.

Most people really don't know what happens to their time. Many times people start their day off with a lengthy list of "to-dos" only to end the day with more "to-dos" than they began with. The time just seems to slip away. That's why I ask my coaching clients to track their time. Although, on the surface that sounds simple enough, it quite possibly is the hardest action plan that all coaching clients are assigned.

In order to thoroughly understand what happens to their time, I ask each coaching client to track their time by documenting the major thing they do in each fifteen-minute increment of their working time each day. I also tell them that no matter how effective or efficient they may feel they are, this will ultimately be an embarrassing exercise (I haven't been proven wrong yet). The reason that this exercise is so embarrassing is that everything they do or don't do with their time is out in the open for public inspection, and there is always waste to be found.

The power in time tracking is that, as I said earlier, knowledge is power. The knowledge of what is and is not happening during the period that was tracked allows each person to make necessary adjustments. Sometimes just a tweak here and there can ultimately be the difference between just being in the game and winning big.

Consider this, if you have ever heard of the Pareto Rule, or the 80/20 rule, you may recall that Vilfredo Pareto discovered that 80% of the people controlled 20% of the money… and, you guessed it, 20% of the people controlled 80% of the money. Pareto also discovered that this principle applies to most every facet of daily life. In the sense of Priority Management, the discovery was that 80% of the results we seek usually come from 20% of the effort we expend. Conversely, 20% of our results come from 80% of the effort we expend.

Therefore, in order to almost double your desired output, you may not have to double your effort. You may only need to discover a way to do more of the 20% that is already giving you 80% of your desired results. In Priority Management, we find that the most effective way to do that is to develop (and live by) a time block.

A time block is simply a hard copy plan for investing your time. King Solomon once said there is a time and season for everything. If that's the case, and I believe it is, then there is a best (or most effective) time to do the things we need to do in life or business. Those things are called *non-negotiables*. The *non-negotiables* are the things that must be done on a daily, weekly, or monthly basis. They represent that 20% that gets you 80% of your desired results.

The trick is to set aside, or block time to do what actually gives you the best return for your time. We call those "high pay-off" activities. Champions intentionally invest their time in those things that give them the best opportunity for success. Champions invest their time on purpose, and since that is not always the easiest thing to do, they commit to be accountable to someone for how they invest their time. Champions are accountable to invest their time wisely.

Championship Living Ingredient #5
Champions seek accountability

The first coaching session that I conduct with a new client is a two-hour session. During that two-hour session we discuss accountability. For many, although they are already successful and have engaged in coaching to raise the bar of their level of success, accountability is a new endeavor. At some point during the conversation I tell them that accountability means different things to different people. Some people need heavy accountability while others do just fine with a much gentler approach. Then I pop the big question. "Which do you prefer?"

The question is not whether they will be held account-able, but rather what type of accountability normally works best for them. I coach accordingly. The fact is that they will be held accountable; the only question is how that account-ability will be applied.

Accountability at its Best

Todd Duncan tells one of my favorite stories of account-ability. He tells this story about himself. To understand the depth of this story you need to know something about Todd. Although I can't say enough good things about Todd, I'll try to be brief. Todd goes first-class in everything he does, from start to finish. He is also a man of his word.

He tells people they need a coach and he backs it up by having a coach himself. One day, in a conversation with his coach, he committed to work out at least four days each week. With his travel schedule it is often difficult to keep that commitment, but somehow he does. However, there was one week that he had only worked out one time and had a coaching session scheduled for the next day.

Being a man of his word, he wanted to keep his commit-ment, so he did the unthinkable. He walked into the gym and did one complete workout, then walked out of the gym and directly back into the gym and completed workout number two. By this time, as you may imagine, others in the gym were wondering what exactly this man was up to; but it gets better. After the second workout, he walked out of the gym again and right back in for workout number three.

He had kept his word and was ready for his coaching session the next day. At some point during the call his coach asked the question: "Todd, did you workout four times this past week." Promptly and emphatically Todd proclaimed, **"Yes, I did!"** He followed that statement with: "…but I will never do it that way again." He told his coach exactly what he did and how embarrassing and painful it was to do three complete, consecutive workouts.

The lesson was learned. As always, he would keep his word, but he wasn't going to allow it to bring him that much pain and embarrassment again. Had it not been for accountability, he would probably have only worked out one time that week. However, because of the accountability, and his character, he did the additional workouts and is probably in the best shape of his life. Todd Duncan is a champion! Todd Duncan practices accountability!

Accountability can be a tool to help you do what you know you need to do, live according to your time block, or remain focused on your vision. It can also be used to resist temptations. For example, Stephen Arterburn and Fred Stoeker wrote a fascinating book titled *Every Man's Battle*. In that book they address how men can win the war on sexual temptation one victory at a time. According to some statistics, pornography is one of the strongest, yet seldom discussed life-controlling addictions that men face today. The only way out for some champions who have kicked the addiction has been accountability.

In a recent coaching session, one client revealed to me that he had faced this addiction in his life and defeated it through ongoing accountability. He joined a group of men in an accountability group that allows for the other men in his group to see every web site he has visited over a period of time. The host for this service actually scores the Web sites in terms of danger or potential danger, and the men actually discuss why they visited sites that could be very dangerous for someone trying to fight this addiction.

The big win for him is in knowing that when he is tempted to open a questionable site, his accountability partners will ask him why he did it. So, at that point he has to ask himself why he wants to enter that site. Accountability helps keep him free. He remains a champion because he seeks accountability. He has a team on his side.

Championship Living Ingredient #6
Champions embrace the team concept

In 1988 I joined an organization that had embraced a new idea in the field of manufacturing called "Team Concept". Today, the term "Team Concept" is widely used to the extent that I believe it is overused. I believe, however, the term is overused because of the reality of the power of a team concept.

I have read that "T.E.A.M." is an acronym for "Together Everyone Achieves More". Although that is true, champions don't take it at face value. They understand the gravity and challenges of working with a team as I learned in those early days in the late 80's. One of the first things we learned is that, although we were operating under the flag of "Team", there still needed to be a clear understanding that every team has a leader.

Those early days were full of challenges because we were traveling down roads that had just cleared the day before. Today, there are volumes of books and courses to attend in the area of Team Concept, but for us, we knew where we wanted to go, but there was no detailed road map to guide our way. There was a lot of trial and error. However, as Robert Frost wrote, "We took the road less traveled by, and that made all the difference." We discovered that all champions have a team, and all the challenges associated with playing on the team are well worth the effort.

It's easy to talk about teams in sports like baseball, football, and basketball, but what about bicycling? There has been so much attention given to Lance Armstrong in recent years that many fail to realize the important roles his team played in all seven of his Tour De France wins. Lance, however is quick to point out that it is not just about him.

Lance Armstrong has a Team

Although there are many stories about Lance Armstrong, the one that really stands out in my mind is the one about a rainy day when Lance was doing some mountain training. On that rainy day as most riders decided to stay inside and to not train in the rain, Lance decided that the rain would not prevent him from training on that mountain that day. He knew that it was possible that it could rain on race day, the day that he would be riding a mountain like that.

As he rode through the rain up that mountain, he paid close attention to the details of that ride; details such as how he was feeling, the timing, and the amount of energy he was exerting. There were, however, certain aspects of that ride that he couldn't measure without the help of his team. Back at training base, medical doctors examined his heart rate at certain points in the training ride that day. Upon return to the training base, Lance was presented with the medical reports of the ride as well as medical opinions about those results. He then could make informed decisions about how to alter his training and strategy for the race.

There are three key components that give Lance Armstrong the opportunity for victory in every race he enters; they are: 1) Lance himself (of course), 2) his equipment (the bike, etc.), and 3) The Team. Without the team it would only be Lance Armstrong and the bike; and that is not a winning combination because there would be a missing link. Like any other champion, Lance Armstrong needs a team to win.

Gentlemen Start Your Engines: Behind the Scenes

One of the fastest growing sports in America is NASCAR racing. If you have ever been to a race you have seen fans wearing tee shirts and caps in support of their favorite drivers. Yet, it's not just the drivers who win races. *Racing teams* win races. Racing is not an individual sport. Although the driver gets the accolades, and a good piece of the prize money, there are many others involved in the race that make it possible for the driver to win.

If you have ever watched a pit-stop crew during a race you know there are several people involved in the effort. Each member of the team has a specific job that is done according to a practiced procedure squeezed into a very short period of time. There is actually a competition that scores teams based on the time it takes each team to carry out certain tasks. One posted time I saw was 16.823 seconds to change four tires and fill the car with fuel. I have read of one team that even broke the 16-second mark in a competition.

Now imagine the driver having to do all of that by him/herself. I doubt four tires could be changed within 16 minutes, not to mention filling the tank with fuel too. How can that be done in 16 seconds? Teamwork is the only answer—a team that is highly trained and focused on the task at hand.

Timing is not the only issue when it comes to the services rendered by the pit crew. Safety is a preeminent life-and-death issue. What if, during the race, the pit crew broke the 16-second record only to see one of the tires separate from the car on a turn? That would be disastrous!

Like the driver, champions know they can't be everything to everybody, every time. They can't do everything by themselves. They know that it takes a well-trained, focused team. It takes the help of others to help us achieve our highest levels of potential. In the Bible, there is a verse that states that a cord of three strands is not easily broken. What a statement about teamwork!

Teamwork and Steel Cord

Early in my career, I worked for a manufacturing company that produced steel wire for steel belted tires. Part of our process was to produce constructions of strands of steel cable wrapped around other strands of cable. One very important quality measurement was that of tensile strength. Tensile strength is a measurement of the capability of tension. As part of our testing, we would clamp the ends of a piece of the construction with special clamps and pull it until it broke. We measured tensile (or breaking) strength by doing that. It became apparent that a construction strand of three cords had a higher tensile (or breaking) strength than the combined strength of each individually.

Champions know that if it works for steel cord, it most certainly works for people. You've heard that two heads are better than one and this is often true. A person who thinks he is the stand-alone champion of the world at any endeavor is set up for failure. Our wise friend Solomon once wrote: "Pride goes before destruction, and a haughty spirit before a fall." This has played itself out time and time again throughout history. True champions are on top, but they aren't boastful. Champions have accomplished more than pretenders, but they know they didn't do it alone; however, they did do their part to get there.

Championship Living Principle #7
Champions Continually Develop Self-discipline

Jim Rohn once said that discipline is the bridge between thought and accomplishment. So many times people have great ideas but don't have the self-discipline to carry them out. That's why Jim said that discipline is the bridge between the initial idea to do something and the actual accomplishment of that endeavor. Victories don't just happen. They occur because proactive action is put in motion to make them happen. I could wish for something all day long, but if I don't get up and do something about it, all I have at the end of the day is an unfulfilled wish.

On several occasions, when I have presented this material, I have made the statement that I believed that everyone in the room was a disciplined person. That's when I would get funny looks like: "I know you're not talking about me, because I am not disciplined." It is fun to watch the "lights go on" when I tell them that I would venture to guess that everyone had brushed their teeth within the past forty-eight hours. Of course they had.

I continue by guessing that, at least at some point in their lives, someone had to remind them to brush their teeth. All heads nod in agreement. The fact is that all of us have areas that we are disciplined in now that we were not disciplined in before. We learned to be disciplined in those areas.

If that is true, then why can't we learn to be disciplined in other areas as well? Well, we can if we want to! It just takes the decision to do it, and the fortitude to stick to it. Saying that you are not a disciplined person is simply not a true statement; it is merely an excuse. Champions don't make excuses. They make positive changes and those changes bring about desirable results.

One of my favorite stories I have heard concerning discipline involves Jerry Rice. As you may already know, Jerry Rice is one of the most prolific receivers ever to play in the NFL. He has earned his "Hall of Fame" status.

During the off season, his workout consisted of two workouts, morning and afternoon; two hours of cardiovascular work in the morning and three hours of resistance (weight) training in the afternoon. However, it wasn't always that way.

Jerry Rice was not a born champion; he did not automatically become a disciplined person. During his sophomore year of high school he would often play hooky from school. One day the principal of the school was about to apprehend this school-skipping-soon-to-be- champion. As he tried to sneak up on him, Jerry heard him coming and sprinted out of sight. As you can imagine, this didn't make the principal very happy. The next day, Jerry Rice was summoned to the principal's office where he met face-to-face with the one he had sprinted away from just one day earlier. This meeting resulted in a couple of completely different outcomes. First, Jerry had to deal with an episode of corporal punishment which, although it is not permitted in school today, created a lasting memory with Jerry's backside that helped him remember that skipping school didn't always turn out to be a good thing. It was the second outcome of being almost caught, however, that may have changed Jerry's life forever. After administering the corporal punishment, the principal promptly notified the high school football coach of the evasive speed possessed by Jerry Rice. As history and fate would have it, the football coach convinced Jerry to play football.

Still Jerry wasn't the disciplined champion that he was about to become. That turning point happened a little later. One of the favorite workouts of the football coach was to have his players sprint up and down a hill fully loaded with equipment (uniform and pads) twenty times. This was no small hill; the distance from bottom to top was forty yards. Obviously this was not one of the favorite pastimes for high school football players; Jerry Rice was no different.

Growing up in Mississippi, Jerry Rice was accustomed to the humidity. In the South, we call it "air you can wear." There are days you feel that the humidity is so thick that you could almost swim through the air. It also drains you of energy. On those hot summer and early fall days, just walking around the block can be an energy-zapping event. Still Jerry was expected to sprint up and down this forty-yard-long hill twenty times!

One day, after hill sprint number 11, Jerry decided that was enough. Nothing in him wanted to sprint those final nine times up and down the hill (so he thought). After scoping out the opportunity to dismiss himself from the sentence of running that hill 9 more times, Jerry discovered that he could get away with just blowing it off and skipping the balance of the hill runs for that day. As he started back to the locker room, he was surprised to discover that there really was something inside of him that would compel him to run that hill nine more times.

It was a voice that said: "Don't quit!" Taken back by the urge to turn back to the hill, Jerry Rice realized that the voice was saying: "Don't quit, because once you get into that mode of quitting, then you feel like it is OKAY." He knew that it wasn't okay to continue with the loser's mentality and follow the trail of defeat back to the locker room. He suddenly understood that there was a better way, a way that would make him a champion. Somewhere deep inside he realized that "Every Day is Game Day" and that he had to live like a champion every day.

He realized that yesterday is gone and there is nothing he could do with yesterday other than to learn from it. He realized the only thing he could do about tomorrow's game on the schedule was to plan for it, and take action today to get himself ready for tomorrow. He realized that the self-discipline he applies today would give him the best opportunity to be a champion tomorrow. Jerry Rice is a champion in the purest sense of the word. Champions continually develop self-discipline.

Champions Apply the Super Seven in Their Lives Daily

Now that you have seen, and better understand the "Super Seven", it's up to you to apply these ingredients for championship living in your life. Today is the day... Today is Game Day! If you don't do it today, then when will you? There will never be a more perfect time than now. It is up to you. If you truly want to be a champion, you will apply the Super Seven. You can begin this process by completing the Power Play at the end of this chapter. For more information on applying the Super Seven Ingredients of Championship Living to your life, visit our Website: www.gamedaychampions.com

In the next chapter, you will see that champions are not pushed but rather drawn by passion and excellence.

Power Plays – Chapter 8

- Develop your own Knowledge Acquisition Plan by listing the areas you would like to gain more knowledge and then expand on that list by adding specific plans for growing your knowledge in each area.

- Review the list of reasons (as stated in the chapter) why people fail to implement consistently and determine what you need to do concerning the ones that consistently stand in your way. Develop a plan of action and involve your accountability partner.

- Log on to www.gamedaychampions.com and click on the Priority Management link to develop your own personal Priority Management System.

- Read *Talent is Not Enough* by John Maxwell

- Read *The Richest Man Who Ever Lived* by Steven K. Scott

- Read the book of Proverbs in the Bible (there are 31 chapters that are best read one chapter each day for 31 days)

CHAPTER 9

Champions are Drawn by Passion and Excellence

———⟨∞∞⟩———

Contrary to popular opinion, champions aren't driven. They don't have to be... they are drawn. People that are driven, for the most part, have to be. They have accepted a life that requires them to be driven by something. When I think of being driven, I think about cowboys in the Wild West, driving cattle across the plains. The cattle don't know where they are going, and really don't care. Still, in herds, they are driven. Daniel Harkavy, founder and CEO of Building Champions coaching company, wrote an article titled *Get Out of the Backseat and Drive to Success*. In that article, he wrote about the fact that some people are moving through life with someone else doing the driving, when all along they could get out of the backseat and do the driving themselves. They could go where they want, not just where they are being driven, if they would only get out of the back seat and get behind the steering wheel. Champions do their own driving; they take responsibility for their own actions and, as Harkavy puts it, they drive to success. They go where they want to go.

Also, contrary to popular opinion, champions are not merely intentional. Too much has been written about living an intentional life. It's really not that big of a deal. I know too many people who are only intentional. They say things like: "I intended to take that action…write that card… speak to that person… or accomplish that goal." I have always heard that the road to hell is paved with good intentions. Although I'm not so sure about that, I am sure that there is a verse in James 4:17 (NKJV) in the Bible that says, "Therefore, to him who knows to do good and does not do it, to him it is sin." Wow! It's one thing to say that being intentional without action can cause major difficulties; it's clearly something else to call it *sin*! If you believe the Bible is God's Word, and I do, then you have to believe that God, the Creator of everything, calls a mere intentional life a life of sin.

So what does all of this have to do with living like a champion every day like it's Game Day? Although champions are clearly intentional, they don't stop there. The word *intentional* as defined by *Webster's New World Dictionary* means *done purposely*. Although, as humans, almost everything we do is done purposely, everything we do is not always according to the purpose of our desired end-result. Let me explain. As I was writing this chapter, my daughter came to tell me that she had found an old videotape of our family at a lake house several years before she was born. My desired end-result for tonight was to write a certain portion of this chapter, but guess what I did? You are absolutely right; I watched the video.

Was it wrong to watch the video? Definitely not! Did I "sin" by leaving the writing of this chapter to watch that video? No way! It was good to invest time with my family. I was given the choice of two good ways to invest my time. However, did the video help me stay on course in getting the chapter written? No. Although I may reach my goal of where I wanted to be in this chapter by the end of the night, it will be at least an hour later than I intended. Oops, there's that word *intended*. You see, the word intentional is derived from *intend* which means *to plan*. I had planned on writing to a certain point and to be finished at a certain time. That plan changed when I made the decision to stop writing and watch the video. I will catch up, but it will have to be at the expense of something.

With everything we say "yes" to, we are saying "no" to everything else for that particular time. I said "yes" to watching that video, and for that period of time I was saying "no" to writing this chapter. At this time I am saying "yes" to writing this chapter, which means I am effectively saying "no" to reading, sleep, etc. Is that good or bad? The best answer I can give for that is the answer my statistics professor gave us in grad school as I was working toward my MBA. He said that, in statistics, the right answer is always "it depends". Although I never tried that one during an exam, to some degree I knew he was right. Was watching the video rather than working on this chapter good or bad? Is writing right now rather than reading something, or sleeping good or bad? It depends. It depends on which choice better plays into my over all long and short term life goals.

I said all of the above to emphasize that we all have choices. We have the ability to choose to drive, or be driven. We have the ability to choose to do one good thing or another. Charles Kaiser, Jr. once said, "The greatest enemy of *best* is *good*." If you're willing to accept *good* you'll never be the *best*. This statement is not in conflict with the verse mentioned earlier that if you know to do good and don't do it, it is sin. It's just a matter of translation. The Greek word used for "good" in that verse is "*kalos*" meaning valuable. In other words if there is something valuable to do, we need to do it. To not do so would be to squander our time, and champions see that as being a sin.

Champions See Further Than the Bottom Line

Profit and Loss, affectionately known as P&L to many leaders, is the daily focus of many business leaders. Too many, however, are driven by P&L to the extent that it obscures other vital issues. True champions are focused on something else, P&E: *Passion* and *Excellence*. With the focus on Passion and Excellence in business, the P&L is more P than L. Profits are high, return on investment is good, and the world just seems right. It works the same way in the personal lives of champions, too.

Champions have learned how to discern between what is merely good and what is best. They have learned to not only be intentional about what is best, but to follow through with taking the best action. They are drawn to what is best with passion and excellence. Let's look at these two words individually.

Champions Burn with Passion

What is passion? By definition, passion is defined as being a strong feeling, the object of a person's strong liking or great enthusiasm. Just a few years ago, Hollywood was taken by surprise with the blockbuster effect *Passion of The Christ* had with movie goers. That "passion" is defined by the suffering of Jesus from the night of the Last Supper until his death on the cross as told in the Bible. Jesus was drawn to the cross, not by a passion or great enthusiasm to suffer, but by the passion or great enthusiasm to do the will of His Father and provide a way of salvation for the world. He was drawn there by passion. What are you passionate about? What do you want so badly that you are willing to suffer to get it?

Passion is also defined as a strong love between a man and a woman. There is a story of passion in the Old Testament that almost makes me laugh and cry at the same time. It's about a man named Jacob and a beautiful lady named Rachel.

Jacob was on a journey and stopped at a well. There were some guys who were about to water their sheep gathered around the well. They were waiting for someone to bring the rest of the sheep so they could take the stone off the well and begin to water their herds. Jacob asked if they were from the area and they confirmed they were. He asked if they knew one of his relatives named Laban and they did. He asked if Laban was well and they confirmed that he was and directed Jacob's attention to Rachel, who was bringing sheep to the well.

Jacob was captivated by Rachel's beauty. He rolled the stone from the mouth of the well himself and proceeded to water the sheep. Then he uttered the ultimate one-liner, one that is sure to get most men slapped; actually it wasn't a one-liner at all... he kissed Rachel! Then he broke the news to her that he was actually one of her father's relatives... talk about kissing cousins. Rachel didn't slap Jacob, but she did run to tell her father.

Laban wasn't upset with Jacob as one might think. Jacob actually stayed with Laban for a month. Obviously Jacob had been doing some chores for Laban, because at a certain point, Laban mentioned that, although they were related, Jacob didn't have to serve him without payment. He asked Jacob what his preference was in terms of wages.

Jacob quickly replied to Laban: "I will serve you seven years for Rachel, your younger daughter." Now I remember when I asked my father-in-law to be for his daughter's hand in marriage, although I was in love, I never considered making an offer like that! But Jacob did and Laban accepted. In fact, Laban said: "It is better that I give her to you than that I should give her to another man. Stay with me."

Jacob served Laban seven years; but it only seemed like a few days to him because he loved Rachel so much. Talk about passion! It was an exciting day when Jacob went to

Laban and said, "Give me my wife, for my days are fulfilled." He had served his seven years and he was ready to marry Rachel. It's what happens next that makes me want to laugh and cry at the same time.

I've never understood how this happened, but somehow Laben gave Rachel's sister, Leah, to Jacob in marriage rather than Rachel. Jacob didn't even know it until the next morning. Apparently Leah was wearing the world's thickest bridal veil, and they skipped the part about "you may now kiss the bride". That's what I call a bait and switch!

Jacob went to Laban and said: "What is this you have done to me? Was it not for Rachel that I served you? Why then have you deceived me?" Laban simply looked at Jacob and said: "It must not be done so in our country, to give the younger before the firstborn." He then told Jacob that if he would serve him seven more years he could marry Rachel. What would you have done?

One word that can describe what Jacob did is *passion*. He served Laban seven more years and then married Rachel. Was he crazy? I don't think so; he was just that passionate about Rachel. After he served those fourteen years to marry Rachel, he stayed and served Laban seven more years. That must have been some first kiss!

What are you so passionate about that you would gladly do double- duty to achieve? What swells your heart with enthusiasm to the extent that you are drawn by that passion? Champions find the answer to that question and they are fired with a Jacob-like passion and are willing to pay the price to make it happen. When you have a vision that makes your heart beat faster, you will pursue that vision with passion. You will be drawn.

Champions Accept Nothing Less Than Excellence

As I was growing up, I remember my dad telling me something that his mother told him as a child: "If a task is once begun, never leave it till it's done. Though the labor be great or small, do it well, or not at all." She was telling him to live by a code of excellence. Choose wisely the tasks that you start, but then finish what you start. She was also telling him to either do what he chose to do well or never start it. She was describing what it was like to focus on excellence. Two words come to my mind when I think about this saying; "Finish Well".

Best-selling author of *Half Time*, Bob Buford, recently released his newest book titled *Finishing Well: What People Who Really Live Do Differently*. In the book, Buford shares that it is never too late (or too early) to begin finishing well. He interviewed 61 people such as Peter Drucker, Jim Collins, Dr. Kenneth Cooper, George Gallup, Howard Hendricks, Roger Staubach and Bill Pollard. The common theme is that these people live(d) lives of excellence. They are fixated on excellence.

Excellent people lead excellent lives. Champions live excellent lives. I have a client, named Rodny Davidson who has developed a phenomenal approach in his sales business. He has been praised for his accomplishments. Rodny has shared his system with several people I know and the two responses that I get over and over from people that I have introduced him to are: 1) "Wow, what a nice guy!" and 2) "He seems down-to-earth just like me!" I can't help but wonder what people expected. Although he is an awesome guy (I would love to tell you that it is all because of my coaching but then I would be exaggerating) he is just another guy who has figured out how to live life like a champion. He has determined to live every day as if it's Game Day because it is. Rodny lives by the principle of living every day like a champion. He has earned his way to the top of his field; he knows that he has to live that way every day because it is the only way for champions to live. He is not driven, but drawn by Passion and Excellence. Rodny Davidson is just an average guy who has a passion to be focused on excellence. Champions are just average people who are focused on excellence every day.

You see, champions are in the same battles as everyone else, they just fight differently. Sometimes it's just the mere fact that they keep fighting when others quit. Another client, Donnie Eden, had the fight of his life after he was diagnosed with cancer. Donnie is a champion. He is a husband and father who owns his own mortgage company in middle Tennessee. He sings on the worship team at his church, and coaches people how to run every race from a 5k to a full marathon; but he had to fight to stay alive and then keep fighting to regain his health. It wasn't easy, but he won. He has shared with me that his "Chemo Couch" became a place of reflection and deep thought concerning the meaning of life. Fighting through the treatment was as tough as fighting through the illness. Yet, if you ask him today, he will tell you that the diagnoses and subsequent battle was the best thing that ever happened to him. It has given him a deeper sense of the true meaning of life. Through the battle he learned to fight the good fight. He learned to persevere; he learned to win.

In the Sunday school class I teach, there is a lady named Tracy. One Sunday as I was teaching the class on perseverance, I asked for people to share examples of times in their lives when they were required to persevere. As she raised her hand, I had no clue as to the gravity of the story that was about to unfold. She shared with us that several years ago she had been diagnosed with cancer and began taking treatments. At that time there weren't as many medicines available that could counter the horrible side effects of chemotherapy as there are today. At a certain point she had taken all she thought she could and made the decision to stop the treatment and take the few months the doctor had given her to live and try to live it in as much comfort as possible.

Upon telling her mother of her decision, her mother did something startling, something that ultimately saved her life. Her mother asked her to think about all of the people that she could help if she lived. She asked her to think about the good things she could do and the excellent life of service she could live if she would only fight through the sickness caused by the drugs that were intended to save her life. Then she told her that if she wanted to be selfish and give up, that it was her decision. She just needed to realize that she wouldn't be there for all those people she could help if she lived. No doubt, rocked by her mother's statement, she decided to fight. She decided to do what she could so that she would have the chance to live a life of excellence in service. She won that battle, and today she stands as that person her mother told her she could be. Had she given up, she wouldn't have been there to tell that story to our class, and you wouldn't have read it in this book. She chose excellence over ease.

Obviously, some people fight as hard as others and still lose the battle. It's not always how hard we fight the battle of sickness. Sometimes it's just our time to go. I firmly believe that, through poor choices and bad habits, we can shorten our days. I also believe that with good choices and good discipline we can live a richer and fuller life. The key here is that we should fight with all we have in us to live a rich and full life, and when that day comes that we exit earth, we will know that we have given it our best shot.

Two Types of Battles Everyone Faces

Every human being, champions included, faces two types of battles. They are: 1) The Battle to Avoid that which is not Needed, and 2) The Battle Not to Avoid that which is Needed. Although those two battles may sound redundant, they represent critical areas that are overlooked by many.

Battle #1
The Battle to Avoid That Which is Not Needed

Like everyone else, some of the battles champions fight, have to do with avoiding things that they think they want to embrace, but know they need to avoid. Sometimes they may initially want to give up, while at other times they may want to give in. However, when they realize the consequences of such actions, they arm themselves for battle and choose the excellent way.

Michelangelo was famous for many works of art, but one of the most impressive was his sculpture *David*. Once when asked how he carved such a marvelous sculpture, he replied that he just started with a block and carved away everything that was not David. In the end, there was David. If you have ever tried sculpturing you will know that it isn't really that simple, but then again, maybe it is. Sometimes it is more important to know what to edit from your life than it is to know what is needed and how to add it to the mix. In some areas, you can just chisel pieces of yourself that are substandard and do not befit a champion and wind up being amazed by the champion that remains. I truly believe that everyone has a champion within... sometimes it's just a matter of recognizing that fact and cutting away everything else. A verse in Hebrews 12:1 (NKJV) says it all: "Let us lay aside every weight, and the sin which so easily ensnares us, and let us run with endurance the race that is set before us." Galatians 5:7 (NKJV) says, "You ran well; who hindered you from obeying the truth?" It's easier to run in this race we call life without being hindered if we lay aside all that slows us down. What is it that you need to lay down? What slows you from revealing the champion within?

There are certain foods that champions avoid, not because they dislike the food, but because they dislike the end-result of eating that food. There are certain vices that champions avoid, not because they are not tempted to give in to those vices, but because they know that those vices will not produce the excellence in their lives that they want more than the moments of pleasure they provide. Excellence, therefore, is not an easy choice or a simple way to live. It's tough, but well worth it. Excellence is a way of life for champions.

Battle #2
The Battle Not to Avoid That Which is Needed

Co-mingled with the battle to avoid certain things is *The Battle Not to Overlook That Which is Needed*. Champions aren't immune to the fact that, just like everyone else, they face the challenge to do what they need to do. In other words, as Pat Williams writes in his must read book: *Who Wants to Be a Champion?*: "Successful people hate to do the same things that failures hate to do. The difference is that successful people make themselves do what they don't like to do. The failures wait for someone to make them do it." It's not just the failures of the world who fight that battle… they just lose that battle more often than champions.

Why do champions win this battle more often than failures? The answer to that question may be found in the title of this chapter, *Champions Are **Drawn** by Passion and Excellence*. Champions are actually drawn to do what they initially didn't want to do. They are inspired. I was recently coaching a client who told me that his wife had told him that she couldn't figure him out when it came to motivation. She reminded him of the disdain that he had for athletes that had all the talent in the world but didn't play like a champion.

She had seen him prevail, and she had seen him fail, but she couldn't determine what caused either one. After some discussion, he realized that he was not passionate about his goals. For various reasons, he just didn't get excited about his own vision. Finally we discovered the source that was squelching the vision. We eliminated that distraction and he began to see his goals through a fresh set of eyes. Although the jury is still out, I expect to see some major gains in this area of his business. He wasn't drawn before and now he is.

Passion and excellence are twins that push each other to the brink of astounding success. When passion is present, excellence is soon to follow. As more excellence is exhibited, the passion grows... Passion and excellence are the dynamic duo in the life of a champion. They promote growth in one another which results in championship living. Consistent championship living produces results beyond your wildest imagination.

This book is an illustration of how passion and excellence worked together to promote the creation of *Every Day is Game Day*. First there was a spark, then a little flame, then a full-blown passion within me to write this book. In my mind's eye, I visualized readers applying the principles to the extent that they would become champions in their own lives. This fueled the passion and I started to write, seeking excellence in the product. So I wrote, and re-wrote paragraphs. Just as Michelangelo chipped away at that block to reveal *David*, I became immersed in my art. My progress unleashed more passion to keep writing.

At a point, I started using the material in speaking engagements with clients all around the country. During one week a few months ago, I presented a portion of this material in New York and L.A. in the same week. On Wednesday, I presented to a group of about 50 people in New York, flew to L.A. that night, coached regular coaching clients over the phone from my hotel room in L.A. then presented to a group of sales people the next day. The response was tremendous; the passion produced excellence that fueled more passion to add more excellence to the book. Passion and excellence go hand-in-hand to raise the bar even higher. I am hooked on passion and excellence. I am drawn by passion and excellence.

Death to Mediocrity!

In the *Merriam Webster's Collegiate Dictionary*, *mediocrity* is defined as being "the quality of state of being mediocre with moderate ability or value – a mediocre person". Now that should be the goal of everyone we know... let's all be mediocre people, living mediocre lives with mediocre passion to live more mediocre years on this mediocre planet. Not me! If you know anything about biology or physics, you know that this planet is not mediocre, it is a very special place created perfectly for human life, like no other planet we know. I have no desire to live any more mediocre years, although I've lived a few because of poor choices on my part. I know I'm not a mediocre person, and neither are you. In fact, according to Psalm 139:14 (NKJV) we are "fearfully and wonderfully made"! The human body is an amazing thing! So I have absolutely no desire at all to live a mediocre life. That's just not what I am called to do. However, I have been given the ability to choose between the two: living a life of melancholic mediocrity, or a life of passion and excellence. I exercise my right to choose every day because in the game of life **Every Day is Game Day!**

Faulkner's Words of Wisdom

Author William Faulkner, during his Nobel Prize speech in 1950, said: *"I believe man will not merely endure, he will prevail. He is immortal, not because he, alone among crea-*

tures, has an inexhaustible voice but because he has a soul, a spirit capable of compassion and sacrifice and endurance."

Obviously, Faulkner knew that man does not win every battle, nor will he live forever on this earth. So what was he saying? In the phrase: "man will not merely endure, he will prevail", I believe he was recognizing the battles that we all fight while living on this earth. He also recognized the difference between enduring and prevailing, and realized that we have the capacity to **prevail** and not merely just **endure**. He delineates the distinction between merely enduring and prevailing when he notes that man has "a soul, a spirit capable of compassion and sacrifice and endurance." Endurance provides a means for us to "carry on"; we need that. We can never prevail if we don't endure. However, victory, or the ability to prevail, comes from the potential for compassion and sacrifice.

Consider those two words: compassion and sacrifice. *Compassion* is defined as sympathetic consciousness of others' distress together with a desire to alleviate it... the word literally comes from the root word *passion*. *Sacrifice* is the act of surrendering something for the sake of something else. It truly takes sacrifice to live a life of excellence. We literally have to sacrifice the status quo, the way we have always done things, if we want to live a life of excellence. I believe Faulkner was sharing his own philosophy for successful living. First we must endure, and then we must have compassion and sacrifice to lead the lives that we are called to live... because we have been given the spirit to do so.

Gripped By Passion and Excellence

When you are gripped by the power of passion and excellence there is no room for mediocrity. A life of mediocrity is a boring life. It leads to a life of poverty, not just in terms of monetary deficiency but also in the quality of one's life. Mediocrity regenerates itself. When that happens, both passion and excellence are cast aside. As a result, people living lives of mediocrity usually become people driven by negativity. They are driven by the woes of the day, the fear of tomorrow, and depression. Failures are driven to places of pessimism and regret. Champions, on the other hand, are drawn to unknown places of enlightenment, passion and excellence.

There are certainly two unknowns, one of indescribable beauty and one of unknown torment. In a sense, it's like heaven and hell. No one on earth knows the full beauty and tranquility of heaven, and no one knows the complete darkness and emptiness of hell. There are, however, people who know that heaven is where they want to be someday, and hell is a place to avoid.

Champions proactively take a grip on their own lives and deal mediocrity a death sentence. No longer will they be pulled down by the gravity of mediocrity, which kills the drive for excellence. They take control and do what they are capable of doing to eliminate the effects of mediocrity in their lives. They don't do anything half-heartedly. They either do things whole-heartedly or not at all. They are resolute in their desire to totally destroy *average thinking*. Rather then being driven by something else, they are drawn to passion and excellence every day in every way. They understand there are no shortcuts on the road to success. Consistently living every day as if it's Game Day produces within them more passion and excellence. They become perennial champions... and you can, too!

The Power Plays at the end of this chapter will help you with passion and excellence. In the next chapter, you will see that the table is set for Goal Attainment – The Breakfast of Champions. "Come and dine" might be the best way to invite you to Chapter 10.

Power Plays – Chapter 9

- Log on to www.gamedaychampions.com to read Daniel Harkavy's article *Get Out of the Backseat and Drive to Success*

- Are you reviewing your Life Plan and Business Vision on a regular basis? If so, do they ignite passion within your heart? Are you excited about the future? If not, review the process, schedule another day to find your passion and allow it to flow into your Life Plan and Business Vision. This is all about your heart. The focus should be on your desired end result.

- Document, in your Champion's Journal your biggest struggle in Battle #1 as stated in the chapter.

- Do the same for Battle #2

- Document your plan to consistently win these two battles. Who is holding you accountable?

- List any areas in your life or business where you are not operating with excellence. Determine the appropriate disciplines and accountability needed... add these to your working list of action plans (things to accomplish by a certain date).

-Read *Who Wants to be a Champion* by Pat Williams

-Read *Half Time* and *Finishing Well* by Bob Buford

CHAPTER **10**

Goal Attainment: The Breakfast of Champions

⎯⎯⎯❊⎯⎯⎯

Goal attainment: what beautiful words they are! It just feels good to say those words. They are akin to saying, *"Mission accomplished,"* with a slight distinction. "Mission accomplished" has a much larger connotation than "goal attainment." Think about it like this. In 1980, during the Olympic gold medal hockey game, with 8:39 to go, the USA national hockey team scored a goal to tie the Soviet Union. The team had been working to attain that goal for some time in the game. However, tying the game was not the objective, or mission, of the team. It was their mission to win the game. Only after they won that game could they say "Mission Accomplished". We addressed the overall mission of a champion in Chapter 3: Champions Live Every Day with Purpose. That's the mission, and as long as there is breath in the life of a champion, there is still a mission (or purpose) to accomplish.

This chapter is about the goals it takes to complete the mission and how to achieve those goals. In that unlikely finish to win the gold medal in 1980, it took more than one goal to accomplish their mission. Before that game it took multiple goals spread over multiple games that had to be won to get to the gold medal game. So the team had to score enough goals in the game, and prevent the opponent from scoring as many goals to win each game. Winning each game became the goal to get to the next one, and the next, so they could "go for the gold."

It goes back even further than that. Each player on the team had the goal of first making the team, then making a positive contribution to the team during practice and during individual games. So there may be numerous goals that add up to the positive outcome of "Mission Accomplished". In order to better understand the process of "Goal Attainment" we must first consider the anatomy of a goal.

Goal Development

A goal, by definition, is the "end toward which effort is directed". At first I wanted to argue with *Webster's Dictionary* (how silly would that be?). I thought there needed to be more explanation than that. There are a lot of "ends toward which effort is directed" that are not positive. I could invest the rest of this chapter just to name and expound on a few. So how could the definition of the word goal include that? It took me less than thirty seconds to realize that I did have the appropriate definition for the word goal, I was just thinking about it in one dimension.

During Life Planning coaching sessions, many times I will mention that although people don't aspire to mess up their lives, very few have a preventative plan that keeps them from doing so. As previously stated, people invest more time planning a holiday meal then they do planning their lives. Although that's true, I had never thought about the fact that goals are goals, be they positive or negative. Notice there is nothing in the definition of the word goal that gives any reference to the word intentional. It just states that a goal is "the end toward which effort is directed".

While coaching priority management, many times I mention the fact, as we discussed in Chapter 9, that every time they say "yes" to something, they are immediately saying "no" to **everything** else for that particular moment. None of us can be in two places at the same time. Therefore, whenever a person chooses not to take action proactively, he is opting for another path that leads him to an undesirable destination. Thus, he is making the conscious decision to pursue a different goal. In the end, the "goal" that is reached is unfulfilling. With that in mind, maybe a more appropriate title for this chapter would be "Intentional Goal Attainment: The Breakfast of Champions".

So, **how are appropriate goals set and met?** What an excellent question! Everything we have discussed in this book has led up to this question. Everything! It's only after you discover your purpose and cement the vision that you can fully understand what goals should be set and what disciplines are needed to achieve those goals. But since you are this far into the book, you must have done all of that pre-work to goal setting. With that done, you are ready to set goals and start acting on the plan to bring them to pass.

Let's begin with a new definition of the term "Champion's Goal". *A "Champion's Goal", by our definition, is a specific word picture of the intentional desired end-result of an action or set of actions proactively taken to obtain that desired end-result within a specific period of time.* That may be a mouthful, but we can easily break it down to its components:

A Champion's Goal is:
A Word Picture...

Too many times, people keep their goals in their heads. However, a goal can just be something swirling around in the grey matter between your ears. There's just too much going on in there already. It must be written on paper or some electronic form that is easily accessible.

Think about it, how many times have you ever walked into a room only to forget why you were there or what you had come into that room to get? If you're like me, the number is too many to remember. But when that happens, what is the natural course of action? Go back and retrace your steps. Although you may not understand why, something happens within the synoptic connections that allow you to remember why you came into that room in the first place. The same principle applies to goals. If your goals are not written down, they are easily forgotten. Busyness takes the place of good goal attainment business.

Therefore, a goal is a picture painted with words. You have heard that a picture is worth a thousand words, and I have found that to be true. So, there is power when we paint that picture (or goal) with words. As you read the word *orange*, my guess is that you probably have an image or picture of the fruit in your mind. The sense of the smell of citrus in the air may have also entered your mind. That's just how powerful a word, or group of words, can be. Whoever, said, "sticks and stones may break my bones, but words will never hurt me", in my opinion, would have to be a deaf person who can't read. Words build up, and words tear down. In writing a "Champion's Goal" you must be very particular as you develop the wording of the goal so that it consists of a grouping of words that build up and inspire rather then tear down and break the spirit. Consider for a moment these words of Solomon from the Bible:

Proverbs 12:18 (NKJV)
There is one, who speaks like the piercing of a sword,
But the tongue of the wise promotes health.

Proverbs 18:4 (NKJV)
The words of a man's mouth are deep waters;
The wellspring of wisdom is a flowing brook.

Proverbs 25:11 (NKJV)
A word fitly spoken is like apples of gold
in settings of silver.

Proverbs 18:21 (NKJV)
Death and life are in the power of the tongue,
And those who love it will eat its fruit.

It seems to me that the wisest man to ever live had quite a bit to say about the power of words. The words we say are important; so are the words champions use when they create the word pictures of their goals.

Goals should always be written in the positive present tense. That means that the goal should be written as if it were a statement of fact. When a goal written in the positive present tense is read, the subconscious accepts it as fact and begins to work on making it happen. That's why affirmations are so powerful. There is a psychological term known as structural tension that addresses this powerful phenomenon. Structural tension occurs when you connect something visual to your goal so that every time you see it you trigger the impulses in your subconscious mind to think about the goal. For example, I have a certain amount of money that I would like to donate to charity during a certain time period.

Without mentioning the actual amount of money, there is absolutely no way it will happen under current circumstances. Therefore it is what we in coaching call a Mount Everest Goal or MEG for short. I needed a way to remind myself of the goal every day, so writing a check for the exact amount that I want to give and placing that check in my wallet in front of the currency was an idea. Now, every time I open my wallet to retrieve currency, I see that check. Although I don't always actually read that check, I know that it is there and at least subconsciously think about my goal. This structural tension is strategically placed to remind me of my goal multiple times daily. This only serves to reinforce the synoptic connections within my brain and stimulate creativity and subsequent action.

Champions write their goals and find ways to remind themselves of those goals. It is important to note that even the process of writing a goal is an integral part of goal attainment. Although it all starts in the heart of a champion, it is essential that goals be written. Written goals are word pictures that stimulate the brain to see fruition of the goal. Written goals get acted upon; unwritten goals often are procrastinated and easily forgotten.

Goal Assertion or Affirmation

An affirmation is simply a statement that asserts something has been validated; it also serves as a statement of dedication. So, in this sense of the word, an affirmation is a statement of dedication to assert what is written is (or will become) valid or confirmed.

There are also times that the power of affirmation works in reverse. Actually, it's not that it is working in reverse; it's just that people affirm the wrong things. I have heard that some people actually talk themselves into being sick. Self-talk is powerful. Consider again the words of Solomon when he says: "You are snared by the words of your mouth; you are taken by the words of your mouth." Proverbs 6:2 (NKJV). People are actually snared by what they say. Sometimes what people say (and think about themselves) is actually influenced by what other people say about them.

Horse Sense or Horse Hockey

At times people even take unconscious cues from other people and take what they say as true. One of the strangest stories I ever heard about unconscious clues involves a horse by the name of Clever Hans. In 1911 Stumpt and Pfungst, two researchers began an investigation of this horse named Clever Hans that could supposedly perform mathematical calculations. According to some, the horse could respond to math questions with the correct answer. The Clever Hans' owner, a German mathematician named Von Osten, would ask the horse to solve addition, subtraction, multiplication and division questions and Clever Hans would respond with the correct answer.

Astonished by the observation of Clever Hans correctly answering mathematical equations, the quest of many became to discover the "trick". This was tough, the horse could actually correctly respond to questions even when the owner was not in the room. However, through some observant investigation, it was determined that the Clever Hans could only respond correctly to questions if two variables were in place. He had to be able to see the person asking the question, and the person asking the question had to actually know the correct answer to the question himself.

How could that possibly make a difference? Why would it matter that Clever Hans could see the person asking the question? What difference did it make that the person asking the question knew the correct answer? The answer was an amazing discovery! Somehow, Clever Hans was picking up on unconscious signals the person asking the question was sending as they were expecting the horse to respond to their question. The point of this story is not to focus on the fact that a horse could detect the cues from people asking questions, but that the fact remains we all to some extent take cues from other people. Champions have learned how to distinguish between the cues that will promote their goal attainment activity, and those that don't. They use to their advantage the ones that do and discard the ones that don't.

For example, while in high school, I wanted to participate as a writer on our school paper "The Trojan Torch". The only way to be on the school newspaper staff was to get a letter of recommendation from an English teacher. I'll never forget the day that I asked for that recommendation. My teacher told me that he would write something for me, and I was thrilled with that. However, the day came to pick up the recommendation and deliver it to the student editor of the paper. Curiosity overruled better judgment and I read the letter of recommendation written by my teacher. It said something to the effect of, "I recommend Tim to a menial position on the *Trojan Torch* staff."

I had the recommendation that I had wanted, but what did that word menial mean? What type of position was he recommending me for? After some quick research, I learned that *menial* meant *insignificant*. A quick check of the thesaurus revealed that menial was just another word for unskilled, boring or basic. He had just recommended me to the lowest position available on the school paper staff!

I would be lying if I told you that didn't affect me. It did! It almost set me back; I almost gave up and didn't do it. I was, maybe not just unconsciously, taking a cue from someone else that I wasn't a skilled writer. Suddenly it occurred to me that this person didn't know anything about me other than what had been accomplished in English class; and that was rather menial. I realized that my thought didn't really matter. The effort, or lack of effort, that I was putting forth in English class that year had earned me a "menial" spot on the school newspaper staff. Being thankful for the opportunity to participate, I was not satisfied with a "menial" position. From that day on, my course was set to improve my writing skills.

Champions pick up on the cues they are getting from outside sources, but they realize that becoming (and remaining) a champion is an inside job. I read the cues from my English teacher, but it didn't knock me out of accepting the position. It made me want to fight—not fight my English teacher, but fight myself, the one who had been taking a lazy approach! I wrote that year, and the next, and the next, and am still writing today. Champions hear the crowd but realize that it is just noise. They don't get overly excited with either the accolades or the lack of confidence offered by others. Their objective is goal attainment!

The Environment and Approach of a Champion

Champions are subjected to similar challenges that "ordinary people" face; they just choose to respond differently. There is no doubt that environment affects us, but champions don't allow their environment to be their adversary. They assess the environment, make whatever adjustments are needed, and then proceed on the course to victory. In realizing that every day truly is Game Day, champions realize that the environment is only one element that factors into their approach. It is just part of Game Day.

Think about it like this. In golf, there are 18 holes that must be negotiated. In this case, the term negotiated means that golfers must adopt a strategy for playing each hole; on a golf course there are no duplicate holes. From the tee, foremost in the golfer's mind is the approach to the pin. Just in case you are a non-golfer, the pin is the flag that is standing in the cup... and putting the ball in the cup is the objective. Along the way from tee-to-pin, there are areas with such ominous names as the rough, out of bounds, sand traps and water hazards. Every golfer knows that the goal is to reach the hole in the fewest strokes possible; however, the quickest way to the hole is a matter of individual choice.

There are two basic styles of approach: the one champions take, and the one everyone else takes. Although no one wants to be caught in one of those "traps" I mentioned above, many people allow their focus to be on avoiding them while champions focus on something else. Champions focus on an area I haven't mentioned, the fairway. The fairway is the "trail" to the pin. It's on the fairway that the grass is cut shorter and there are no trees or obstacles along the way. It's the ideal path to the goal.

Of course, champions understand the "dangers" associated with the environment of a certain hole of golf and they do adjust their game to avoid areas other than the fairway. However, rather than lending their focus to the "traps" along the way, they focus on an area in the fairway where they want their ball to land. The Law of Self-Fulfilling Prophecy tells us that if we focus on avoiding the "traps", many times that's where the ball will go. The sub-conscious does not understand the word "don't", so when the focus is "don't hit the ball in the trap", the sub-conscious hears, "Hit the ball in the trap." So that's where it goes many times. The focus of a champion is different. He focuses on positive outcomes.

I have been guilty of taking the negative, or "don't hit it in the trap" approach before, and the result was the same almost every time. The ball found its way to the trap. Let me share one non-golf story that happened to me. I mentioned earlier that I played on a softball team. During that time, I developed an "approach problem" and it cost me some serious embarrassment.

I was the second baseman and not many balls got by me. There were many games that, when the game was on the line, I wanted the ball to be hit to me. A ball hit anywhere close to me was a sure out almost every time. Although I can't explain what happened, something happened. A ball was hit to me; I caught it, and threw it right over the first baseman's head. To make it worse, our first baseman was every bit of 6'5" tall... and in slow-pitch softball the bases are only 65 feet apart! That was embarrassing enough, but it got worse!

Although it wasn't every ball thrown to first base that went wild, there were plenty. It got so bad that every time I caught a ball, I would say to myself: "Don't throw it over his head!" There were times that I didn't, and I threw it in the dirt in front of his feet! Very few balls hit the mark, and what was once a fun game turned into a nightmare. I even tried changing positions. There were times I would play either shortstop or third base just to have a different angle or perspective. Although that helped, each time I tried to move back to second base it would happen again. It was all in my head. The funny part was that when a play developed very fast and I didn't have time to think, the throw was always on target!

Notwithstanding, the concept of a champion's approach and the power of the sub-conscious, the only approach I knew was to focus on not making bad throws. After making too many, I convinced myself that I needed to change positions; not exactly the champion's way. I would love to go back and take a different approach, the champion's approach, but I can't go back; and I no longer play in an organized softball league. Yesterday is gone, the only thing I can do is learn from it, and that is what I have done. Today I take the champion's approach.

The Champion's Approach:
Relating the Sub-Conscious and Self-Conscious

Champions understand that it is not the environment's fault if something goes wrong; it's the self-chosen response to the environment that is sometimes the problem. Champions make good decisions in the conscious many times because they planted the right seeds in the sub-conscious. Let's take my example of bad throws. I had been feeding my sub-conscious to accept the fact that focusing on not throwing the ball over the head of the first baseman would help. I didn't understand how the sub-conscious worked. I didn't achieve my goal of throwing the ball to the first baseman because all my sub-conscious heard was "make a bad throw", and many times I did.

So, why were good throws made when the play developed fast? It was because I didn't sub-consciously think about not making a bad throw. I instinctively did what had been done successfully in the past. Although it is amazing that the sub-conscious is so powerful, champions have learned how to consciously control their sub-conscious.

While in college, I started majoring in computer science to become a systems analyst thinking that was what I *wanted*. I convinced myself that was the thing to do. It was amazing to see all of the career profile results point to the "assumed" fact that I should be a systems analyst. After taking several courses, I really wanted to do something else. However, the powerful lesson was that I had consciously re-programmed my sub-conscious to believe that I needed to be a systems analyst to the extent that career profiles I took pointed in that direction. That was an epiphany for me!

If it worked that way, would it work in reverse? Could I actually take control and consciously affect my sub-conscious, or was the self-conscious totally left to the devices and controls of the environment around me and totally out of my control? Are the sub-conscious and self-conscious states of mind related or connected in some way? In order to better understand the relationship of these two different states of mind, let's take a deeper look at each.

Let's consider the self-conscious first. *Self-conscious-ness*, as defined by *The Dictionary of Psychology* is: 1) oversensitivity over one's behavior, 2) awareness of one's own mental processes, and 3) awareness of one's own existence as a unique individual. The first part of that definition is the one that I have heard associated with self-consciousness most. It really has a negative connotation because of the oversensitivity involved. It's one thing to be sensitive to one's behavior; we all should do that. However, it's not mentally healthy to be oversensitive to our own behavior.

At Building Champions we use the DISC Profile to help us better communicate with our clients as well as to help them communicate better with those they associate with on a daily basis. DISC is a very accurate and powerful tool, but without going into great detail on the dynamics of DISC I will only focus on one component part. The DISC profile assesses the natural and adapted states of behavior as they relate to the 4 parts of DISC (Dominant, Influential, Steady, and Compliant). In the comparison of the adapted and natural states, we always find that adaptation is always present. However, what we don't want to see is a vast amount of variation over an extended period of time. I believe God created us to be able to adapt our behavior to various situations, but when we do it over an extended period of time we are drained of much needed energy. So being oversensitive to our own behaviors and reacting to them over an extended period of time will zap energy right out of a person, just like a hot and humid day in the South will completely drain one.

Although oversensitivity to one's own behavior is the first and most widely recognized definition of self-consciousness, it's the latter two definitions that get my attention as they relate to a champion's process of attaining goals. The second and third parts of the definition refer to a person's awareness of his/her own mental processes as well as the awareness that she/he is a unique individual. This flies in the face of the environment in and of itself producing behavior. To me, it's clear that as unique individuals, it's something other than the environment that makes us unique. Along with that, "the awareness of a person's own mental processes," means that there are mechanisms that control the mind that can and do reach the realm of awareness. If that is so, then it lends itself to the idea that one has some control over his or her own mental processes. One part of that mental process is what goes on in the sub-conscious.

It's in the understanding of the sub-conscious that champions begin to feel they are in more control of a greater part of their brains. This is extremely helpful in the consideration of goal attainment. Again, as defined in the *Dictionary of Psychology*, the sub conscious is, as 1) derived "in Freudian nomenclature, a transition zone through which any repressed material must pass on its way from the unconscious to consciousness, 2) descriptive of processes by which the individual is not aware but can be brought to consciousness (many memories would fall into this class) and, 3) pertaining to what is in the margin of attention; pertaining to that of which one is only dimly aware."

The key words and phrases in that definition include *transition zone, repressed material, processes*, and *margin of attention*. The definition refers to the "transition zone through which any repressed material must pass on its way from the unconscious to consciousness. This raises some very interesting questions. How did the material get repressed? What causes the transition? What are the processes that can bring this material to consciousness? How does that which is in the margin affect us? How can we affect it?

In his wonderful book, *Who Are You Really And What Do You Want?*, author Shad Helmstetter, Ph.D. writes: "A curious, but important, fact of the human brain is that it is designed to accept whatever we put into it – whether what we put into it is true or not!" He goes on to say that: "The comparison of the success mechanism in our brain to the programming of a personal computer is not only accurate, but also clear: it tells us exactly what we need to do if we want to succeed. – Until our personal internal computers are programmed with exactly the right success programs, they will not help us be successful – they can't!"

We can actually program and re-program what is in our sub-conscious. It has been said that our sub-conscious controls many of our actions and reactions; however, we know today that we, as conscious individuals, actually have a lot of control of what is planted in our sub-conscious. Champions understand that what we once thought had a lot of control over us is almost completely controlled by us! Champions use this control, or ability, to program their sub-conscious in their efforts of goal attainment.

According to Helmstetter, with the help of medical computer imaging technology, the programming process at work in the neuron structure of the brain can be watched. He assesses that no longer is it just theory, he states that it is "medical and neurological scientific fact." In the book, he even gives a ten-step summary of how the programming process works. In one step he states, "…messages we receive are actually physically recorded, chemically and electrically, in the neural pathways in the brain." Champions understand that when they get this right, goal attainment is merely the manifestation of planting the right seeds and having the discipline to follow through. They use the knowledge of this process to enhance their chance for goal attainment.

From Substantial to Sustained Goal Attainment

It has been well documented that there are endorphins released in the brain when goals are achieved. An endorphin is a natural chemical that enhances a feeling of well-being. It can almost be like candy, and most of us have succumbed to that childlike lure to candy when it comes to endorphins. Let's look at one example. Whenever a task is completed and can be "checked off" the "to-do" list, endorphins are released and that good feeling of accomplishment engulfs us. Are you *endorphin-experienced*? I bet you are? Have you ever added something to a "to-do" list just so that you can check it off as being completed? Most of us have, and the reason is that it feels good to attain or accomplish goals.

It's a good thing to want to experience that feeling, but there is a danger. The danger is that we might tend to gravitate toward the easiest goals or tasks on the list just to get that endorphin rush quicker. Champions take another approach; they prioritize their goals and do their best to accomplish the goals of highest priority first. Although they are lured into the pull of the endorphin rush, they stay on task, and that task is to accomplish their goals according to their priorities.

After each high-priority goal is accomplished, champions do something else before moving on to the next. They endeavor to standardize the process or method that allowed them to reach the goal in the first place. Although it takes a little longer to stay with an already achieved goal to standardize the process or method, champions understand that it is worth the time invested.

Fun with Numbers

Early in my career, I worked in a privately owned commercial bank. My position was accounting clerk in the comptroller's office of the bank. My duties included balancing correspondent bank statements, tracking teller daily differences, and developing the income and expense statement of the bank on a monthly basis. At first, I realized that it was very tedious; one mistake early in the process could cause several hours of additional work just to find the error. This was also a very lengthy task. The entire report was done on a 14-column pad, not exactly high tech. If done right, with no errors, it could take up to four hours to complete.

The goal each month was to get it done quickly and correctly. Needless to say, those two rarely worked in tandem. Believe me, whenever the report was completed and verified that it was correct, there was a rush of endorphins. One day the comptroller (now bank president) told me that he thought this task might be made simpler by using some new computer software affectionately known as Lotus 1-2-3. Many reading this book may not even remember Lotus (it was the predecessor to Microsoft Excel and other spreadsheet programs).

With his permission, I began the quest to first learn Lotus 1-2-3 and then develop a file that would help us decrease the chance for error and speed up the process, thus bringing into tandem the two former archrivals— accuracy and speed. Although it took a while, after learning Lotus, the file was developed and we were ready for our trial run. It was a huge success! We actually completed the perfectly accurate report in less than twenty minutes with the added benefit of having a crisp and clean report as the result! Gone forever were the errors and hours of labor. Gone forever was the dread of doing that report... but that wasn't the end of the story.

We needed to standardize how the new report was administered each month and create a back-up system. We had to be able to replicate the success we had just achieved so the process could be repeated over-and-over each month. That was accomplished and others started to notice what we had achieved. This led them to think of other ways that Lotus could be used in their areas. Soon a bank wide PC (Personal Computer) task team was formed and I was asked to be the lead-person in that group.

The beauty of the story is that the comptroller's idea became a reality, a goal was set and accomplished, a system was developed to replicate the success, and others in the organization benefited from our work. We had moved from a *substantial* attainment to *sustained* attainment. A four-hour, arduous and tedious task was reduced to a swift twenty-minute walk in the park.

On another occasion, as a coach with Building Champions, I was frustrated with one of our early tools. It was the tool for Business Planning. The tool itself was conceptually sound; however, calculations had to be completed by clients themselves and the reporting process had to be faxed or snail-mailed to the coach. Since snail mail was too slow, most were faxed. Unfortunately, our logo (and I love our logo) was shadowed on the page behind the worksheet part where the calculations were to be entered. As you can imagine, that made for a blurred fax. Even if the faxes were readable, the calculations would need to be double checked since they were not electronically done.

Remembering the days of Lotus and the monthly bank income and expense statement project, I considered developing a tool that could be calculated electronically and e-mailed to the coaches as an Excel file. Thinking about redeveloping the tool, I considered combining it with a tool that was developed by our vice president of coach development, Barry Engelman. That tool was called *Navigator*. We agreed, and work started. It was time to learn Excel and that was easy enough. The goal was to create a business-tracking tool that would serve the needs of our clients. Upon completion, we had a tool that quickly became a favorite of our coaching clients. This occurred despite the fact that the inspiration came from a need to get readable information. The point is, as we set and reach our goals, there are residual benefits for others. Champions understand that substantially attained goals can have positive residual effects as they are sustained.

The Final Word on Goal Attainment

In Proverbs 13:19 (NKJV), Solomon wrote: "A desire accomplished is sweet to the soul…" Goal attainment is the breakfast of champions; it is sweet to the soul. One major difference between champions and failures is that champions persevere in the quest for goal attainment while failures drift away. As goals are set and the journey to goal attainment begins, there is an air of excitement. Aspirations abound at the thought of pursuing goals. As time passes, however, that excitement has a tendency to ebb. Days, weeks and sometimes months go by after goals are set and the original excitement dims. Sometimes the Law of Diminishing Intent kicks in to the extent that the effort toward goal attainment erodes into uninspired activity. That erosion of effort produces negligible results. At that point goal attainment becomes a distant memory.

This happens less to champions because they keep their focus on the goal. They keep the goal in front of them at all times, and they constantly think about how to "record the win." They also act on those thoughts. It's the sweetness to the soul that they long for as their desires (or goals) are accomplished. Goal attainment truly is the breakfast of champions, and that breakfast gives these winners the sustenance to live on purpose.

Power Plays – Chapter 10

- Write 3-5 affirmations based on your Life Plan and Business Vision. Find a way to keep this list close to you at all times and read it often.

- Review your goals. Do they paint the picture you want to see in life and business? If not, re-write the goal(s). Make sure the goals have a target date for completion.

- Make a list of the intentional "cues" you have established to promote attainment of your goals. Are these "cues" working? If not, develop new intentional cues.

- Re-read the section on "The Environment and Approach of a Champion". Consider your own environment and approach to goal attainment. Is it conducive to the attainment of your goals? If not, determine the changes that need to be made, and make those changes.

- Listen to Jim Rohn's recording of *Goals* (see link at www.gamedaychampions.com)

- Consider following Jim Rohn's One Year Success Plan (see link at www.gamedaychampions.com)

- Read *Who Are You Really and What Do You Want?* by Shad Helmstetter

CHAPTER **11**

Champions Live a Life of Fulfillment

—⚬⚬⚬—

It would be easy to write a chapter patterned after the Tim McGraw hit song, *Live Like You Were Dying*, a song that very well could be the theme song for living every day like it is Game Day. This chapter is about living like you are *alive* and intend to stay that way for a long time! To live like you were dying could mean the focus is on the fact that the end is inevitable. *Living like you are alive* suggests that, although we all know we are mortal, we must live our lives as if the lives of others depended on our living like a champion every day. Living every day like it's Game Day is not about an end, but rather a process— a process designed to bring fulfillment in the short- and long-term.

Therefore, to live like you are alive carries with it the thought that we are to focus on the present as we plan for the future and learn from the past. Living like you are dying has to do with finding closure with only a short period of time left. Living like you are alive has more to do with current activities and new beginnings as well as closure or fulfillment of purpose.

In the Bible, one of the main characters was a man named Paul, and at one point Paul contemplated this very issue. Paul was a Christian; he understood his purpose in life was to follow Jesus Christ and to promote His teachings. He also believed that with all of the suffering he had experienced in this life, that for him to die was actually gain. He had been beaten and imprisoned on several occasions, yet he believed that there was a reward waiting on the other side of his earthly existence. He believed that reward would far outweigh his present sufferings.In his writings to a church in Philippi, he stated: "For I am in a strait betwixt two, having a desire to depart, and to be with Christ; which is far better: Nevertheless to abide in the flesh is more needful for you." (Philippians 1:23-24 NKJV) What he wanted was relief from the arduous task at hand, but what he set his mind to do was to fulfill his purpose. Some people live to get by, while champions live to have a richer and fuller life. Mark Twain once quipped, "Let us endeavor so to live that when we come to die even the undertaker will be sorry." My uncle, Jerald Hamm, did just that. Although it is sad that we may never live to see our legacies played out on stage, they (legacies) are there for all to see after we are gone. During his lifetime there were occasions that we, his family, got a glimpse of his legacy, but it played like a feature film at his memorial service. Over 500 people came to show their respects and to share their stories of how he had positively touched their lives.

Ask yourself how many people will testify about how you made a positive difference in the lives of others. Who do you want to be remembered by and how do you want to be remembered? Then ask yourself what you did about that yesterday, what you are doing about it today, and what you plan to do about it tomorrow.

Why is it that so many people run from living life rather than running to it? Why is it so many people know the simple truths that, if followed, can ensure that they are on the right course in life, yet they tend to ignore those truths? Why is it that people know what to do but don't? I believe an important reason is that people don't make it their goal to live every day like a champion. Could it be they just don't care? I believe their apathy is due to a lack of inspiration and focus.

In one of the best books I have ever read on focus, The *Power of Focus*, Jack Canfield, Mark Victor Hansen, and Les Hewitt discuss ten different focusing strategies:

1. Your Habits Will Determine Your Future
   Successful people have successful habits;
2. It's Not Hocus-Pocus, It's All About Focus
   Build on your strengths, not on your weaknesses;
3. Do You See The Big Picture?
   Designing our crystal-clear future;
4. Creating Optimum Balance
   More money, more time off;
5. Building Excellent Relationships
   Your entry into the big leagues;
6. The Confidence Factor
   Eliminating fear and worry;
7. Ask For What You Want
   A seven-point system to help you prosper;
8. Consistent Persistence
   Success is often just around the corner;
9. Taking Decisive Action
   Proven systems for creating wealth, and
10. Living On Purpose
    Making your life simple again.

That inspiring book was written primarily to help you focus on your strengths and eliminate everything that is holding you back. The primary impact of doing that is living a life of fulfillment; that happens by living like a champion every day. Fulfillment usually doesn't come in a day, but rather in the day-by-day consistent pursuit of excellence in everything. Our legacy is really a compilation of stories and we are writing those stories every day.

You are making up your own stories and creating your legacy every day that you live on this planet we call earth. How will your legacy-ledger balance out? What will people be saying about you one day? Better yet, what are they saying about you today? That, my friend, is your choice. Your actions today determine how you will be remembered tomorrow. They regulate the lasting impact you have on the lives of others. Your choices will produce either positive or negative results.

Remember Paul? Remember how he was "in a strait betwixt two desires"? He wanted to depart from this world, yet he knew that he had not fulfilled his purpose. Let's fast forward to the time of his death and consider what he said in II Timothy 4:6-8 (NKJV): *"For I am ready to be offered, and the time of my departure is at hand. I have fought a good fight, I have finished my course, I have kept the faith. Henceforth, there is laid up for me a crown of righteousness, which the Lord, the righteous Judge, shall give me at that day: and not to me only, but unto all them also that love His appearing."* What did he mean by that? Let's look at it phrase by phrase.

"I am ready to be offered"

Throughout this book, we have considered what it takes to live like a champion every day. In chapter two, *Champions Live on Purpose Every Day*, we introduced the fact that purpose begins to come into focus at the point where desire intersects with potential; we discussed the importance of preparation. In this statement Paul is telling us that he is "ready". That word "ready" is taken from the Greek word "spendo" meaning to pour out as a libation or to devote one's life as a sacrifice to be offered. He was "spending" his life for a purpose. Another version states: "I am already being poured out like a drink offering." Think about pouring water out of a cup until it is all gone.

Paul was saying that he was giving everything he had, including every breath, for his calling in life. He not only bought into his calling, he was absolutely sold out to it. He was able to endure beatings and imprisonment simply because he was living for Someone bigger than himself. He could have easily walked away at any point. Are you sold-out to finding fulfillment? Are you ready and willing to offer your life to live out your purpose?

In most cases it doesn't take the actual offering of your life; but you have to be willing to make sacrifices to experience victorious living. In writing this book, although I love what I am doing and I truly believe this book will make a positive impact, there are other things I could be doing. I firmly believe that there is nothing more important that I could be doing at this minute other than writing this book. If I did, that's what I would be doing because that's what it takes to live like a champion every day. Every Day is Game Day! Every minute counts!

That's not to say that everything I do is centered on writing this book. I am first a husband and a dad. I am a son who cares deeply for my own mom and dad. I am a fully loaded coach with clients I love to encourage toward excellence in their lives and businesses. I am a writer and speaker. Writing this book fits perfectly in my life plan, but it hasn't been easy. What I am saying is that sacrifices have been made to write this book and they have been made on purpose.

"and the time of my departure is at hand"

Have you ever been late and missed a flight? There are departure times for planes, trains, buses, and people. Planes, trains, and bus departure times can be missed, but the one departure time that will not be missed is the appointed time for our earthly departures. A missed flight can be a traumatic experience, especially if you have connecting flights that you will also miss. A missed flight can be remedied because there is always "the next flight out," even if that flight is the next day.

As a coach, there are times that my clients prefer me to come on-site with them to make various presentations or to engage in face-to-face coaching with them or their team. Our policy, at Building Champions, is to always arrive the day before, just in case there are delays at the airport. The reason for this policy is that a few years ago, Daniel Harkavy, the CEO and founder of Building Champions experienced a delay caused by heavy fog that prevented his plane to land. As the plane circled, the thought raced through his mind that just a few thousand feet below the area they were circling was a group of people waiting to meet him. There was nothing he could do but continue to circle until the fog lifted and air traffic controllers gave them the okay to land.

In our lives, there is a day and time that we will land. A time has been appointed for us all. However, just as Harkavy didn't know when he would be able to land, we can't foresee when our "time to land" or exit this world will be. Harkavy was not in control of the flight plan, so he was relegated to occupying his time by reading and writing.

What are you doing today? Hopefully you are not just circling as you wait for that day and time of your departure from this earth. Champions want to take advantage of every single minute they have on earth.

"I have fought a good fight"

We all have fights to fight as we make our way through
life's passages; but, in the end, will you be able to say you
have *fought a good fight*? Will you even be able to say you
fought at all?

When I was about ten-years-old, I would avoid a fight at
all costs, mostly because I didn't want to get hurt. Did you
ever encounter a bully when you were growing up? I did.
That bully's name was Terrance (I changed the name, but it
wasn't to protect the innocent). Almost every time I would
play with the other kids in our neighborhood, Terrance would
try to run me away. Most of the time, I would just leave.

Although it's funny now, it wasn't so funny then. You
see, I wouldn't just leave, I would leave crying. It gets worse.
I wouldn't just leave crying, I would go home and literally
crawl into the house my dad and I had built for my dog (I had
a pretty big dog). That's right; I would get in the doghouse!
If you are a guy, and you've been in the *dog*house at home
with your wife, you have a clue as to how I felt. Yet, I was
literally in the doghouse.

One day my dad noticed me coming back into our backyard looking like a whipped puppy and he watched me crawl
into the doghouse. After I stopped crying, I crawled out and
went in my own house. My dad met me at the door and asked
me why I had been in the doghouse. After I told him, he
looked at me quizzically and then said something I never
thought he would say. He asked, "Why didn't you fight
back?" You would have to know my dad to know why I was
so surprised. My dad is a peace-loving man who wouldn't
consciously hurt anyone; but that's what he said.

After getting over the surprise of what my dad had just
told me, I asked him what he meant. He said that he meant
what he said. He told me to avoid a fight if I could, short of

running home crying; but if I couldn't, then stay and fight. That scared me. Although I was afraid to fight, I was ready.

A few days later I was playing in the neighborhood again with a group of kids when Terrance made his move. At the time we were all sitting around talking when out of the blue he looked at me and said: "Hey, boy, did you call me a name?" That was it, this was the moment I had been dreading for days. It was Game Day for me!

With all of the courage I could muster, I answered his question and said: "Maybe I did." As you can imagine, my heart was pounding and my breathing was short and shallow. Believe it or not, my heartbeat has increased a little right now as I think about what happened that day. Terrance responded: "What did you say?"

Now, as if once wasn't enough, I had to say it again. I said: "Maybe I did. What of it?" Where did that come from? Was I getting a little more courageous?

Terrance responded with: "Do you want to fight me, boy?"

I said: "If that's what you want to do, let's do it."

He asked again: "What did you say?"

I boldly repeated: "If that's what you want to do, let's do it."

So, we both stood up and we proceeded to walk into the back yard. We weren't alone; all of the other kids followed us. There was no turning back now.

On the way to the backyard Terrance said something that completely startled me. He said, "Maybe we just need to wrestle." Did he say what I just thought he said? Maybe we should just wrestle? Maybe he's not so tough after all; maybe he is just all talk.

After we made it to the backyard and began to wrestle, I realized that although he was two-years-older than I was, he wasn't that much stronger. I was actually holding my own. There came a point in our wrestling match that I actually got him down and bloodied his nose. What a strange turn of events that was! Although I was surprised at what was happening, I was also caught by surprise by the fact that the other kids were actually cheering me on!

Not that I am a proponent of going around bloodying other kids' noses, but that felt pretty good. When it was over, and I was convinced that he wouldn't pick on me anymore, I let him get up. What happened next was the biggest surprise of the day. Terrance went straight to my house and told on me! To beat it all, he told my dad. You can imagine what my dad told him. Actually it was more like a lesson in "what goes around comes around".

The fact is that we are all faced with opportunities to fight or take flight (by crawling in the doghouse) almost on a daily basis. Too many times people take flight in the fights of life rather than facing them head-on and taking care of business, so to speak. It's funny, but I have learned that I never feel good about myself when I take flight from a fight that I needed to fight. The doghouse just isn't where I was born to live.

I feel best when I stay and fight the good fight. The good fight is different from any other fight. The good fight always strives for win / win. Too many times a fight is seen as the hard way out, when in fact, it may be the only way out. It is not a fight so the other person loses, nor a fight that you personally walk away from with a loss. It is a fight to find a better solution. It's a fight to find a way for both parties to win, if possible.

The good fight is a fight that brings peace. Sure, there are times when people walk away with bloody noses, but the desired end-result is peace. I would have never experienced peace in the neighborhood if I hadn't stood to fight Terrance that day. I think in some strange way he actually respected the fact that I stood up for myself.

What fights are you facing today? What bullies are pushing you around? Sometimes I am my own worst enemy; bad habits are what beat me down. I have to stand and fight the good fight. Most of the time, the good fight is an internal struggle, but one worth fighting. What about you? Where do you need to take a stand and fight the good fight?

"I have finished my course"

Are you familiar with the expression, "Winners never quit, and quitters never win."? There is wise counsel found in that statement. How can you win if you quit? Why would you quit if you really want to win?

People quit for various reasons. Some quit because they were never dedicated to the race in the first place. Some quit because the race gets hard and they don't have the heart to finish. Some quit because they haven't trained properly. Still others quit because they are afraid of failure and, believe it or not, some quit because they are afraid of success. With so many reasons to quit, it's easy to see why there are so few true winners. If you really want to be a champion you must finish the course. Hit a home run! Touch all the bases!

Touch Every Base

The first game of the 1988 World Series between the Los Angeles Dodgers and the Oakland Athletics produced a moment in baseball history that will be long remembered. Before the game started, a young and beautiful Debbie Gibson sang the national anthem; but the minds of Dodger fans were on another Gibson—Kirk. Kirk Gibson had been called on throughout the year to light the fire of the boys wearing Dodger blue, and he had consistently come through in the clutch during the regular season. He severely injured his leg in the League Championship Series just days before the World Series. With two hurt legs he was sidelined and couldn't start in the crucial first game of the World Series.

Gibson was hurt so badly that he wasn't even in the dugout most of the game; he was back in the training room watching the game on television. At one point the television camera scanned the Dodger dugout and Vin Scully, who was calling the game for NBC with Joe Garagiola, made the comment that "Gibson was nowhere to be found."

He said: "It looks like he is out for the night." As Gibson saw the TV scan of the dugout and heard the words of Vin Scully, something rose up inside of him. He picked up a bat and proceeded to hobble to the dugout to tell Dodger manager Tommy Lasorda that he was available if needed. He was telling Lasorda that he wanted to bat.

Gibson had always been known as a gutsy player who could get clutch hits, so Lasorda called on him to pinch-hit. With the knowledge that he was about to enter the game, he went to the clubhouse batting cage to warm up. It has been said that he would nearly collapse with every swing of the bat due to the severe amount of pain in his knee. Yet he had reported for duty and he was going to finish the course.

In the bottom of the ninth inning, behind 4-3 with two outs and Mike Davis on first base, Kirk Gibson was given the nod by Lasorda and found himself about to enter the game as a pinch hitter. As he limped to the plate, he was about to face the absolute best relief pitcher in baseball, Dennis Eckersley, a future Baseball Hall-of-Famer. As Eckersley recalls, it took Gibson a long time to get to the plate and that was just driving him nuts. He was thinking that Gibson is the last out so let's get this thing over with. Eckersley later stated he was thinking, "When you have your foot on their throat (2 outs in the bottom of the ninth inning), you want to put them away."

Eckersley got two quick strikes on Gibson and many thought the game was all but over. It seemed just a matter of a couple more pitches before the Dodgers would go down in defeat with their crippled slugger in the batter's box. The next pitch came and it looked like a good one for Gibson to hit. With one swing of the bat, Gibson connected. The ball came off the bat and… and… and… it was a slow roller down the first base line. There is no way with two bad legs Gibson was going to beat it out for a base hit. Some fans stood to get a better view; still others put their faces in their hands so as not to see the game end that way. Then it happened, that slow rolling ball suddenly veered a little to the right and rolled foul. The game had not ended. Gibson had to hobble back to the batter's box.

There was a strange sensation in the air just before each pitch. Both Dodger and Athletics fans shared anticipation of winning the game with the next pitch. There was a certain co-mingling of emotions. With each ensuing pitch, the game held in the balance.

Soon the count was three balls and two strikes. Gibson's at-bat would win, end, or keep the game alive.

Gibson stepped out of the batter's box to prepare for the next pitch. He remembered the words of the Dodger's batting coach who told him that Eckersley would always throw one specific pitch to a left-handed power-hitter with a full count of three balls and two strikes. That's exactly what he was looking for, and that was exactly what he got. With one swing of the bat, Kirk Gibson not only changed the outcome of the first game of the 1988 World Series, he created a moment in baseball history that helps define the sport of baseball.

The ball that Gibson hit was a high fly ball to right field. If it stayed inside the fence, the Oakland outfielder would catch the ball and the game would be over with the L.A. Dodgers going down to defeat; if it carried over the fence, the home-team Dodgers would win the game with what is known as a *walk-off home run*.

Nearly 56,000 people stood to watch the ball soar over the fence and into the right-field pavilion. The Dodgers had won the game! Kirk Gibson had just written himself into the annals of baseball history! But wait! It wasn't over. The Dodgers had not officially won the game yet—he still had to touch all the bases! Only hours before, Dr. Frank Jobe had diagnosed a sprain of the medial collateral ligament and surrounding tissue in Gibson's right knee from an injury that occurred in the final game of the National League Championship Series. The knee had been injected with xylocaine and cortisone. Oh yeah, that was just the right leg. Gibson was struggling with a sore hamstring in his left leg. Yet, he still had to touch all the bases.

The act of "touching all the bases" after hitting a home run is called a home run trot. Some have even called it a *Cadillac Trot* because some home run hitters turn it into a Broadway production; much like some football players do with their choreographed end-zone celebrations following touchdowns. A key difference is that, although it may seem academic, this celebratory trot is required by the rules of baseball. You have to touch all of the bases; you are required to **finish the course**.

Gibson's trot was more than just memorable. It wasn't a Broadway production, and it certainly wasn't pretty, but it was *classic*. He finished the course; with two hurt legs, he touched all the bases.

Champions touch all the bases in life. They finish the course in spite of internal and external difficulties or challenges. The challenges faced by Kirk Gibson were internal; he could hardly stand on his pain-wracked legs. In 1976, New York Yankee hitter Chris Chambliss faced external challenges in touching all the bases. He had just hit a home run to win the American League Championship for the New York Yankees who had suffered through a dozen years of mediocrity without winning a championship. At the site of the ball sailing over the fence for a game winning "walk-off" home run, Yankee fans swarmed onto the field and met Chambliss half-way between second and third base, showering him with high-fives and pats on the back... the only problem was that he couldn't see where third base was because of all the fans on the field in the base path. Finally he made it around and touched third base and then home plate to seal the deal for the win. For the first time since 1964 the Yankees had won the American League Championship! Chambliss fought through the elated crowd and touched all the bases; he finished the course.

In what areas of your life do you need to finish the course, or touch all the bases? All of us experience times of inconsistency that stand between us and the finish line. Many people are good starters; fewer are strong finishers. Develop a list of those areas in your life where you need to be a strong finisher, develop a plan or course of action to follow through. Make a list of the bases you need to touch... and touch all the bases so you too can own the title of *Champion*!

"I have kept the faith"

What is faith, and why is it important to keep it? Let's look at some phrases that I have heard over the years as they relate to faith:

- "Seeing is believing";
- "I'll believe it when I see it", and
- "Believe nothing that you hear and only half of what you see."

Consider for a minute the conversation between CBS radio announcers Jack Buck and Bill White moments after they had just witnessed Kirk Gibson hitting that game-winning home run. As Gibson was trotting (actually limping) around the bases, Jack Buck exclaimed the following:

"I don't believe what I just saw!... I don't believe what I just saw!... Is this really happening Bill?"

Bill White responded:

"It is happening, and they've gotta help him home... The third base coach Joe Amalfitano had to give him a little push... and all the Dodgers are around home plate..."

Jack Buck said it again:

"I don't believe what I just saw!"

Although we know that Jack Buck really did believe what he just saw, is seeing really believing? Or, is believing really seeing with eyes of faith, even before something actually happens?

How can we believe in something we can't see when, at times, we can't even believe what we see? Have you ever seen a magician trick you by his / her sleight of hand? If you have, then you may believe that "the hand is quicker than the eye"? The truth is that the hand is not really quicker than the eye. Think about it, in a single glance, your eyes can take in everything within the boundaries of your peripheral vision and immediately transmit that sight to your brain.

So if it's not quickness, what is it that allows a magician to fool the audience? I believe it has more to do with focus than speed. A magician will usually do something to draw your attention ever so slightly away from the true point of action just long enough to affect the outcome of what you see. If that happens in the short span of time it takes to perform a magic trick, how could Paul stay so focused on something he couldn't see, to the extent that he could say "I have kept the faith"? The answer is that he kept his eyes focused on the object of that faith; in this case it was Jesus Himself.

Paul's stated: "Therefore we also, since we are surrounded by so great a cloud of witnesses, let us lay aside every weight, and the sin which so easily ensnares us, and let us run with endurance the race that is set before us, looking unto Jesus, the author and finisher of our faith..." Hebrews

12: 1-2a (NKJV). Paul kept the faith because he kept the focus; he was always looking ahead. He was "faithful to the fight, faithful to the faith, and faithful to the finish." (Vance Havner)

In yet another verse he stated: "Brethren, I do not count myself to have apprehended; but this one thing I do, forgetting those things which are behind and reaching forward to those things which are ahead, I press toward the goal for the prize of the upward call of God in Christ Jesus." Philippians 3:12-14 (NKJV) He kept the faith because he kept his focus on what was before him in his quest. In the end, Paul could say in II Timothy 4:8 (NKJV)...

"Finally, there is laid up for me the crown of righteousness, which the Lord, the righteous Judge, will give me on that day..."

Paul ran his race for a crown of righteousness that he believed was laid up for him. Notice his focus was not on himself, but rather on what he believed to be his ultimate purpose in life. As Pastor Rick Warren would say, Paul lived a *Purpose-Driven Life*.

So why are you running? What is laid up for you at the end of today, this week, this month, or eternity? In this book you have been introduced to various principles, guidelines and tools designed to help you find your purpose and then genuinely live according to that purpose every day of your life here on earth. Now it's up to you. The choice to live every day like a champion is just that, a choice... and that choice is yours and yours alone. It's not up to your family, your friends, or your co-workers; it's all on you. It is totally 100%, up to you!

Now it's time to face the music, just like I had to do when I was caught crawling out of the doghouse after I wouldn't stand to fight. It's time that you take 100% responsibility for the results you desire in your own life. Remember, everything you did, or didn't do yesterday affects today. There is nothing more you can do about yesterday than learn from it. Yesterday has already been written in the history book of your life. It's behind you. Today is Game Day... today is the day you can change!

Today is the day to start planting what you want to harvest in your life tomorrow! Today is the day to start applying the *Power Plays* as well as the additional tools available at my Website, www.gamedaychampions.com. You can begin to live the game of your life like a champion. You were created to be a champion... and today is Game Day!

Champions finish the course; they touch all the bases. They know the rules of the game. They know when they have won. They know what it is like to hit a walk-off home run. You can be the champion that you want be; and now, my reading friend, you know more about what it takes to live like a champion. By applying the principles and their accompanying actions revealed in this book, you are on course to live like a champion every day!

Power Plays – Chapter 11

- Review your Life Plan as developed in Chapter 6 and ask yourself if you are really doing what you need to be doing to ensure the legacy you desire. If not, follow the Keep – Start – Stop method of thinking to develop a list of actions you can take by certain dates to make the necessary changes. Make sure you involve your accountability partner… and touch all the bases.

- Consider a time when you were hurt in some way (as Kirk Gibson) and yet you stepped up to the plate and followed through to victory. Journal this event in your Champion's Journal.

- Read *The Power of Focus* by Jack Canfield, Mark Victor Hanson, and Les Hewitt

Chapter 12

You Leave the Legacy You Choose

---∞∞∞---

Reputation and Reality

What kind of legacy will you leave? The funny thing about life is that we will all "leave". We will all leave this earth, and we will all leave behind a legacy. The choice of the kind of legacy you will leave is yours. Nobody else leaves your legacy for you. There are no external circumstances that dictate the kind of legacy you will leave.

The fact remains that, if you died today, your legacy would be set; when you are gone, nothing can change it. The great news is that, if you are reading this book, you aren't gone... it's not over... it's not too late. If you don't like the legacy that would be left if today were your final Game Day, you can begin to change it right now... today! Today is Game Day. The rest of your life starts right now.

I once heard a story of two old friends who sat on the porch every day listening to baseball games on the radio. One day one of the old men turned to the other and asked if he thought there would be baseball in Heaven. After a few minutes of pondering, one of the guys developed a brilliant plan. He said: "I'll tell you what, if I go before you, I'll come back and let you know if there is baseball in heaven… and, if you go before me, you come back and tell me." His porch-sitting, baseball-listening partner agreed and the deal was struck.

On a cold, rainy day in the dead of winter, one of the two men died. While grieving for his friend, the remaining man realized that, if his friend kept his end of the agreement, he would soon know if there were baseball games in Heaven. Spring came and a new baseball season began. Sure enough, while sitting alone on the porch listening to a baseball game, the old man was a bit surprised to see his friend in the yard walking toward the porch. He stood up with excitement and looked at his former baseball partner and said: "Well, is there baseball in Heaven?"

His friend looked at him and said: "I've got good news and bad news for you; first of all the good news. There is baseball in Heaven and we play every single day, there are no rainouts and it never gets too hot to play."

His friend replied with excitement and said: "That is great! …but what is the bad news?" Without hesitation, his partner said: "You're scheduled to pitch this Sunday."

Imagine that, there's even Game Day in Heaven! The fact is that one day your number will be called, your ticket will be punched, you will kick the can… no matter what you call it, some day in the future will be your last, and your days on earth will be ended. What will you leave in your wake? You have the choice to try to forget about it or do something about this issue. If you want to do something about it, the best thing you can do is to review what you've read in this book and then make the determination of how you will live on purpose every day. You can choose to live like a champion every day. When you do that, you will start to live every day not like it is your last, but with a reborn attitude. Sadly, many never come to grips with securing their eternal victories.

You don't have to be that way. You can figure it out right now. You can make the necessary changes to live an abundant life. That's where most people miss it, they *exist*, but they don't really *live*. You are only given one life to live and that's not a play on a soap opera, it's just fact. What are you going to do with the one life you have? First you have to know what you want, and then know what to do about it. You have the golden opportunity to do what you know you need to do now because tomorrow may never come.

I have heard of people, who at the end of their lives wonder if anyone will attend their funerals. Many people, on their deathbed, have made statements to the effect that it never really clicked with them how to live until it was time to die. For many, there is that lingering fear that they never made a difference. That fear surfaces because we are put here on earth for a reason and we need to know that we have fulfilled our reason for being. Only you can make the decision that your life will make a difference. Only you can determine that you will live a fulfilled life on purpose.

There is no patented program for living the life of a champion. In this book, I have done my best to point you in the direction that will give you the best opportunity to live like a champion every day. I can't jump off the pages and make a difference in your life any more than I can leap through the phone line and make a difference in the lives of my coaching clients. It's your life... today is your Game Day. You are the one who can and should be living it like a champion every day!

Now you have new information that you need to put into practice. It has been my intent to both inspire you to want to live like a champion every day, and to give you tools and direction to help you do just that. It is now an issue of the heart... your heart. What are you going to do with today? It's your call. It's your time to act. My hope is that you will choose to...

247

Live well… live long…
…and live every day like a champion because
Every Day is Game Day!

About the author:

Tim Enochs is a Master Coach with Building Champions. He has been involved with coaching since 2001. His clients have included many business owners and leaders from a wide spectrum of industries nation wide. He holds a BBA from the University of Mississippi, as well as a Masters of Business Administration from the University of Tennessee. Along with his vast experience in coaching with Building Champions, he has experience in leadership roles in manufacturing as well as the banking industry. He has been certified to administer 360 degree feedback instruments, DISC behavioral profiles and has been awarded certification at the PHR level in Human Resources. Along with coaching, Tim is in high demand to present *Every Day is Game Day* material from coast to coast and has taught various adult and youth groups for over twenty years. He resides in Tennessee with his wife of 22 years, son and daughter.

Contact Coach Tim at tim@buildingchampions.com

About Building Champions:

A thletes, entertainers and highly motivated professionals of all disciplines know the value of a coach. They have always known that a good coach can make the difference between mediocre performance and outstanding success. This principle is at work in the business world too. With business opportunities at stake, more and more ambitious leaders are working in tandem with professional coaches to learn to scale the heights of their chosen field.

At Building Champions, we offer several types of coaching to meet the variety of needs that business people have today.

The dictionary defines a coach as "a vehicle that moves people forward." While that definition refers to an actual moving object, that's exactly what Building Champions coaches will do for you. When you tell us how you'd like to improve your business and your life, we'll work with you to create a plan to get you where you want to be.

Through our proprietary coaching systems and curriculum, we'll teach you to maximize your time, find a work/life balance, make you accountable to your action plans and clearly define the purpose of your work. Whether you're an executive, manager or producer, your Building Champions coach has one goal in mind for you: To help you to improve yourself so you can build your business in a way that will make you be more purposeful in your business and your life.

Building Champions coaches you on business and on life. You'll receive interactive tools and assignments throughout coaching that will help you reach your goals – the most important of which is our Core Four® program.

The Core Four®

The Core four® is the foundation of our coaching programs. It has been used and revered by thousands of Building Champions clients. This program provides both a roadmap and focus for the coaching relationship.

The Life Plan

The Life Plan is the starting point for all One-on-One Coaching relationships. The Life Plan will help you define what success means for you and help you determine what is most important by creating order in your life. The Life Plan is often the most powerful tool a coaching client will experience.

The Business Vision

The Business Vision is imperative for any business leader. As part of your Business Vision, you'll be challenged to define the convictions, purpose, future vision and major goals for your business throughout the next many years. Many leaders are amazed at how inspired and focused they become by writing their Business Vision.

The Business Plan

This plan will help you to prioritize the activities and events that will ultimately lead to a successful year in business. You'll be asked to define your goals and we'll help you figure out how to meet them through this plan.

Priority Management

This system will have you completely rethinking your entire schedule – both personal and professional. You will be able to identify the habits and disciplines in your business and life that are most important and then schedule those priorities instead of the priorities taking over your schedule.

We know that job responsibilities and demands vary from person to person. That's why we've created several coaching paths. Take a look at the different choices to see which coaching option is best for you. We're also happy to talk with you in person to explain the programs in more detail. Building Champions can be contacted by calling 503-670-1013 on the web at www.buildingchampions.com .